Princess
Charm School

Lisa Delmedico Harris

Lisa Delmedico Harris

Princess Charm School: A Godly Approach to Beauty, Poise, and Righteousness
Copyright @2018 by Lisa Delmedico Harris. All rights reserved.

No part of this publication may be reproduced, stored in a retrieval system or transmitted in any way by any means, electronic, mechanical, photocopy, recording or otherwise without the prior permission of the author except as provided by USA copyright law.
All scripture quotations, otherwise noted, are taken from The Amplified Bible, Old Testament, Copyright 1965, 1987 by the Zondervan Corporation and The Amplified New Testament, Copyright 1958, 1987 by the Lockman Foundation. Used by permission. All rights reserved.
Scripture quotations marked "NIV" are taken from the Holy Bible, New International Version, Copyright 1973, 1978, 1984 by International Bible Society. Used by permission of Zondervan Publishing House. All rights reserved.
Scripture quotations marked "NKJV" are taken from The New King James Version/Thomas Nelson Publishers, Nashville: Thomas Nelson Publishers. Copyright 1982. Used by permission. All rights reserved.

This book is the sole property of Lisa Delmedico Harris. Copyright 2018. All rights reserved.
Book cover, Interior design by the author.

Princess Charm School: A Godly Approach to Beauty, Poise, and Righteousness

This book is dedicated to girls and women of all ages who desire to live their life in a way that would lead others to Christ.

Thank you for your interest in Princess Charm School. For your interest, I would like to give you a FREE Gift, it's my eBook:

Why Charm School

How a Godly Approach to Beauty, Poise, and Righteousness can make a difference.

To Download this FREE Gift, visit:
https://www.princesscharmschool.com/free-gift

Table of Contents

Princess Charm School Guide — 7
Foreword — 11
Why Charm School? — 13

Beauty

Chapter 1	…and God Created Woman	15
Chapter 2	Princess Power!	21
Chapter 3	True Beauty	27
Chapter 4	God and Your Body	35
Chapter 5	God and Exercise	45
Chapter 6	God and Your Skin	51
Chapter 7	God and Your Make-up Bag	67
Chapter 8	God and Your Hair	79
Chapter 9	God and Your Hands and Feet	93
Chapter 10	God and Your Smile	105
Chapter 11	God and Your Closet	113

Poise

Chapter 12	God and Your Posture	131
Chapter 13	God and Your Confidence	143
Chapter 14	God and Your Attitude	151
Chapter 15	God and the Fashion Industry	159
Chapter 16	God and Your Manners	171

Righteousness

Chapter 17	God and Righteousness	187
Chapter 18	God and Your Relationships	193
Chapter 19	God and Your Future	209
Chapter 20	God and Your Health	219
Chapter 21	God and the Virtuous Woman	229
Chapter 22	God and Queen Esther	233
	Princess Beauty Treatments	241
	Princess Prayers	247
	Beauty and the Bible	250
	The 10 Commandments	251
	The Fruit of the Spirit	252
	Princess Review	253
	Declaration of Acceptance	256
	Endnotes	257

Princess Charm School Guide

👑 **PRINCESS BIBLE VERSE**
designed to fit each chapter and encourage scripture memorization

👑 **PRINCESS BEAUTY TIPS**
comments to help the princess enhance her inner and outward beauty

👑 **PRINCESS CONFESSIONS**
designed to fit each chapter and encourage scripture memorization

👑 **PRINCESS PRAYERS**
prayers designed to help guide the princess in her prayer time

👑 **PRINCESS CHALLENGES**
prayers designed to help guide the princess in her prayer time

👑 **PRINCESS JOURNALING ASSIGNMENTS**
designed to encourage the princess to write her thoughts, feelings, and vision onto paper

👑 **PRINCESS CROWN THOUGHTS**
designed as food for thought for the princess at heart

Lisa Delmedico Harris

1 John 2:6

be an imitator of Christ

"Whoever says he lives in Christ [that is, whoever says he has accepted Him as God and Savior] ought [as a moral obligation] to walk and conduct himself just as He walked and conducted Himself."

Lisa Delmedico Harris

Forward

"The sparkle" I call it. It's that extra twinkle you see in a person when you first meet them. Lisa Delmedico Harris had that sparkle twenty years ago when I first met her, and she still has that sparkle today. Along with that sparkle, she has a lot more—determination, beauty, and the desire to instill in girls of today. The same ambitions and wishes she had as a young Oklahoma girl arriving in the big city—beauty, personality, intelligence, grace and a love of God—made Lisa standout from the crowd. Now she is passing along all of the wonderful nowledge she has to you, the reader of this fantastic book.

As a former student and protégée, this book touched me because I know from my more than forty years of working with young girls and teaching good grooming and etiquette skills, this book can make a difference.

The knowledge in this book comes from Lisa's experience. But this book is more than knowledge; it is from her heart. It provides guideposts to instill value and caring back into your life along with pointing out the power of one realizing that each person has the same powers with the help of God and hard work.

Let Lisa's soul grab you and let her love of family, God, and the genuine beauty found in daily life create a "sparkle" in you.

Susan Huston
Etiquette Instructo, Dallas/Ft. Worth

Lisa Delmedico Harris

Why Charm School?

To truly understand why I have written Princess Charm School, I think it is important that you first know the meaning of charm school. Charm school has been around for many centuries. It was proper for a young lady to attend a charm school in order to learn the correct ways of social graces. Charm schools taught proper etiquette, good grooming, and acceptable social behavior. Etiquette is an extravagant word for knowing how to govern social behavior, and is often a little sign we use to communicate with others. Etiquette helps us get along with other people in our society. Some think that social graces are only for the upper class and not intended for everyone, but that is not the case. Etiquette is for everyone and should be an important factor in everyone's behavior no matter what gender, age, or background. Although etiquette has been lost in our society, it hasn't changed throughout the years.

Princess Charm School was written to help you understand the importance of etiquette and using social graces in everyday situations. There are ways the world expects you to act and get along with others, but they are not always the right ways. God tells us plainly in his word how we are to act as his children and as representatives of Jesus Christ. Christians should act and walk as Jesus did in order to become a witness for him. The word of God is full of etiquette tips about how we are to walk, talk, and act. Princess Charm School
explores these tips, and expands on them to help you understand exactly what it takes to be a beautiful woman of God.

I knew nothing about etiquette and charm school until I attended a fashion college in Arlington, Texas. It was during this time I met a special lady who introduced me to the world of proper etiquette and charm school. She owned her own charm school business, and hired me as her personal assistant. I assisted her in charm school workshops across the Dallas/Ft. Worth area and witnessed her teaching and inspiring young girls everywhere. Her workshops included classes on good manners, good grooming, good table manners, and gave an intro to the world of modeling and fashion. She always ended her workshops with a big fashion show celebration. I loved everything about charm school, fashion, and modeling, and I knew one day I would own my own charm school business, teach etiquette, and inspire young women to be the best they can be.

In 2005, I started Princess Charm School and was inspired to write about and teach etiquette. Princess Charm School combines everyday social graces with godly views. I am glad you have decided to take the charm school journey with me.

My prayer is that you will:

*Let God use the teachings in this book to help you see the beautiful woman he has created you to be.

*Discover your untapped, hidden potential and pursue the will of God for your life.

*Truly know the meaning and importance of true beauty.

*Desire to apply proper behavior in your everyday situations

"The Bible tells us the steps of a righteous man (or woman) are ordered by the Lord. Looking back on the path of my life, I can't help but believe God's hand has been creatively involved in every step." I also believe God has lead you to this book Princess Charm School: A Godly Approach to Beauty, Poise, and Righteousness. He has a wonderful plan for your life. He loves you. Trust Him

Royal Blessings,

Lisa Delmedico Harris

Chapter 1

...and God Created Woman

"God created man in his own image. God planted a garden eastward in Eden, and there he put the man whom he had formed. The Garden of Eden was a wonderful place, but it was missing something to make it complete. It had to be created at just the right time.

Something needed to be specially designed and wonderfully crafted to make it a place of completion.

Now the birds of the air and fish of the sea and all the creeping things on the earth had a helper comparable to them; but for Adam, there was none comparable. And Adam gave names to all the livestock and to the birds of the air and to every [wild] beast of the field; but for Adam there was not found a helper suitable for him.

And the Lord God caused a deep sleep to fall upon Adam; and while he slept, he took one of his ribs or a part of his side and closed up the [place with] flesh. And the rib or part of his side which the Lord God had taken from the man he built up and made into a woman, and he brought her to the man.

Then Adam said, "This [creature] is now bone of my bones and flesh of my flesh; she shall be called Woman, because she was taken out of a man."

Therefore, with God's wonderful brilliance, he took female out of male and created woman. Finally perfection was in the earth, and man had someone to complete his life and bring beauty into it, just like the birds of the air, the fish in the sea, and all of the creeping things on the earth. God's plan was completed, and woman was created to play an important role in his plan.

Women have been uniquely designed from the beginning, and God has touched each one of them with his beauty, his brilliance, and his uniqueness. Women were made to be beautiful. When a woman looks into a mirror, she should see a reflection of God's beauty staring back at her. Too many times a woman loses sight of her beauty by continually focusing on her flaws. Every woman wants to change her appearance and be something she is not. All women have been crafted differently in looks, color, and in the size and shape of her body. No woman has been created perfectly, except for Eve. Eve was created perfectly and placed into the garden. God doesn't produce imperfections or make mistakes. Eve made a choice to trade her perfected beauty for the price of a forbidden fruit. Because of Eve's choice, women continually strive for perfected beauty.

A woman should never criticize the way she has been made, for each woman is God's handiwork. When a woman criticizes the way she looks, she is simply saying to God, that she doesn't approve of his decisions, his plans, or his ideas. Don't pattern yourself to fit the image of someone else. By doing so you are forfeiting your unique beauty. Only observe others from a distance, and never allow yourself to duplicate another. You are too priceless as an original to be reduced to a cheap copy.[1]

You are of great value to God, and your unique beauty has been created to touch lives. Recognize your self-worth, and understand you were not born a woman by accident, but on purpose. He will help you become all he has created you to be. See yourself as God sees you: a brilliant and beautiful woman.

Discover the truth in God's Word and learn what he thinks of you, what he wants to do for you, and what he has already done for you. Don't be afraid of being a woman. Capitalize on the beauty and uniqueness God has given you. Be proud of yourself. Dare to love whom you are, and strive to be a woman of true beauty and excellence. Dare to be the woman God has created you to be, and when it is all said and done you can say, *"and God created woman, and that would be me."*

 ***Princess Bible Verse:***

Genesis 2:7, 18, 21, 23
she shall be called Woman

"⁷And the Lord God formed man of the dust of the ground, and breathed into his nostrils the breath of life; and man became a living being. ¹⁸And the Lord God said, "It is not good that man should be alone; I will make him a helper comparable to him."²¹And the Lord God caused a deep sleep to fall on Adam, and he slept; and He took one of his ribs, and closed up the flesh in its place. ²²Then the rib which the Lord God had taken from man He made into a woman, and He brought her to the man. ²³And Adam said: "This is now bone of my bones and flesh of my flesh; She shall be called Woman, Because she was taken out of Man.

Princess Prayer:

Lord, help me to embrace the fact that I am a woman, and that you knitted me first in your thoughts and then in my mother's womb. Sometimes it is hard to be a woman. There are many challenges, but I am up for them all because I know your plan for my life is far greater than I can see. My prayer is that you teach me how to be the virtuous woman you speak of in Proverbs 31. Help me to become a beautiful woman in your sight so that I can become a more beautiful woman in the sight of others. In Jesus' name, Amen.

 Princess Beauty Tips:
There is beauty in being a woman of God. A princess never allows herself to be someone she is not. She understands her position and the responsibilities that come along with it. Being a woman will take hard work and dedication to maintain inner and outward beauty. Let your princess beauty shine!

 Princess Confessions:
I am a woman, a beautiful creation, and I will embrace it.

 Princess Challenge:
Place a picture of yourself in plain view as a constant, daily reminder that you are a beautiful woman created by a beautiful God.

 Princess Crown Thought:
You are special and beautiful. Think of yourself as the beautiful creation you are. You are a masterpiece created by the wonderful and artistic abilities of God.

Princess Journaling Assignment:

Write down your likes and dislikes about being a woman. Make a list of how you can plan your choices and daily decisions to become a more beautiful woman.

_____

_____

_____

_____

_____

_____

_____

_____

_____

_____

_____

_____

_____

_____

_____

_____

Write Your Own Prayer:

Chapter 2

Princess Power!

The crown of royalty comes with power and authority. You could call it princess power. God has given his children the power of love. In fact, God is love. He is the author and finisher of it. 1 John 4:16 reads, "God is love, and he who dwells and continues in love dwells and continues in God, and God dwells and continues in him." If you continue in love and walk in the power of it, you will be unstoppable. Love is a powerful force that holds the universe together. It completes life and brings about happiness and contentment into the hearts of people. People search for love every day. It is what holds them together. It is what has created each of us from the beginning. Love allows you to see things differently. It gives you the power to love the unlovely, and even love yourself. Many women do not like who they are, and would never think it right to love themselves. But it is right to love who you are. Love brings about a self-confidence that no person or material thing can give. When you love who you are, you are powerful—full of princess power!

There is power in love, and only God's love can bring about that power. You cannot expect to love yourself and to love others in a healthy way until you first know how to love by God's love. God wants you to be kind, gentle, and loving all the time, especially toward yourself. You treat others the way you treat and respect yourself. If you do not respect yourself, others will not respect you. If you cannot love yourself, you will not be able to love others the way God intended you to love. Without the power of God's love operating in your life, you will not be able to walk in love and in victory in all that you do. If you have the power of God's love flowing in you, then his love can easily flow out of you. God's love is more than enough. In our natural mind, it is hard to comprehend why God loves us so much, and why he desires us to be complete in it. But there are many benefits that come along with having God's love.

"I pray that out of his glorious riches he may strengthen you with power through his spirit in your inner being, so that Christ may dwell in your hearts through faith. And I pray that you, being rooted and established in love, may have power, together with all the saints, to grasp how wide and long and high and deep is the love of Christ, and to know this love that surpasses knowledge—that you may be filled to the measure [with] all the fullness of God."

Ephesians 3:16-19 NIV

Princess, when you are filled with love, you are filled and flooded with God himself! It is our responsibility as a child of God to learn about his love through his word. God's love is deep, wide, high, and long and there is no way we can fully comprehend it except through the Holy Spirit. It is amazing to know that God loves us so much that he gave his only Son to die for our sins (see John 3:16). Would you give your life for a friend or family member? Jesus did. Although he knew we would sin and fall short of his glory along life's journey, he laid down his life willingly and shed his precious blood so we could be forgiven. God's love is sufficient, it never fades away, it never leaves or forsakes us, and it is always forgiving of our sins. Through his unselfish act of love for us he has given us hope and power.

In II Timothy 1:7 the Bible tells us, "God did not give us a spirit of timidity (of cowardice, or craven and cringing and fawning fear), but [he has given us a spirit] of power and of love and of calm and well-balanced mind and discipline and self-control." This scripture is proof that God has given the spirit of power and the spirit of love. If you are afraid to love, cast down the spirit of fear, and walk in the confidence and power that God has placed inside you. Fear will cause you to miss the things of God. It will cause you to hold back the true you, and keep you from becoming and receiving all God has for your life. Fear will rob you of your power. By renewing your thoughts with God's thoughts you will find it easy to love and walk in the power of his might. It is not about what you think of yourself, or even what others may think of you, it is only what God thinks that matters. His word says he formed you in the womb and knew and approved of you (See Jeremiah 1:5).

Knowing God approves of you, loves you unconditionally, [and] has given you the spirit of love and the spirit of power, will help you establish a healthy God-image of yourself. Self-image is important to loving who you are. If you don't approve of yourself, how will you have the power to succeed in life? Put your trust in God and his thoughts of you, and he will never fail you. He is a reliant, trustworthy, faithful, and loving God. Don't rely on man's love to fill the void in your life and expect it to make you happy. Man's love will pass away, but the love of God is from everlasting to everlasting. You can love yourself and the people around you.

Healthy love, God's love, will cause you to have personal power, healthy relationships, confidence, and a healthy self-esteem. There is power in knowing and loving who you are in Christ. Begin today seeing yourself as God sees you—a brilliant, beautiful, and wonderful woman worthy of the Father's love. You have the power within to fill the shoes of a princess. Walk in them with confidence, authority, and power.

 ***Princess Bible Verse:***

Romans 5:5

"And hope does not disappoint us, because God has poured out His love into our hearts by the Holy Spirit, whom He has given us."

Princess Prayer:

Lord, thank you for the power of your love. Thank you that you have given me the power to love myself and to love others. I pray that you will open the eyes of my understanding so that I may see and understand the width, height, breadth, and depth of your love for me. Help me each day to walk in your love so that I can be powerful and victorious. In Jesus' name, Amen.

 Princess Beauty Tips:

Nearly every princess has a can of hair spray in her make-up bag. Hairspray is used to keep hair in place. It comes in many different formulas and strengths. We can compare hairspray to the love of God. Like hairspray, God's love will keep you in place and help enhance your appearance. God's love is the only mega-strength formula that will hold you together when the winds of life start to blow.

 Princess Confessions:

I am full of the power of love and will walk in it.

 Princess Challenge:

Wrap your arms around yourself and give yourself a loving hug. Declare, "I love myself and I like who I am."

 *Princess Crown Thought:*

God's love energizes us and motivates us to be all we can be. It gives us the power to love. Man's love will only uplift you for a moment, but God's love will uplift you for eternity.

Princess Journaling Assignment:

Do you like who you are? What are some things you like and dislike about yourself? Why? Examine your thoughts, behaviors, and mindsets not just your outward appearance. How can you improve you?

_____

_____

_____

_____

_____

_____

_____

_____

_____

_____

_____

_____

_____

_____

_____

_____

_____

Write Your Own Prayer:

Chapter 3

True Beauty

What is beauty and why is it so important? The word beautiful in the American Heritage dictionary reads--having qualities that delight the senses (sight); excellent; wonderful[1] and in the Latin language, the word beauty comes from the word *"bellus"* meaning good. Everywhere we look, we are bombarded with images of beauty. We see movie stars, models, and pop stars on TV, in magazines, on billboards, and in the movies. Their beauty is always in our sight, but the beauty that is given to us through the media is an unrealistic form of beauty. No one can look beautiful and perfect all the time. But society makes us believe it is possible.

Being beautiful is a wonderful thing; some portray more physical aspects of beauty than others, but the fact is, we are *all* beautiful in our own special way. Not everyone is born to be a supermodel or movie star. Human nature is attracted to beauty by what our sight brings to us, but by letting our eyes rule our thinking, we allow our mind to make false opinions of beauty. True beauty comes from within the heart of a person. Once you look past someone's appearance, you will see through to another person buried within. Beauty is a state of godliness, not a state of worldliness. Beauty can only be measured by what lies in one's heart.

It seems as though the beautiful girls get all the guys, all the good jobs, all the awards, and all the attention. But we do not realize that outward beauty can be a form of deception. What you see is not always what you get. What lies in the heart of a person holds the true meaning of beauty. Everyone has different degrees of beauty because not everyone is the same on the outside. However, everyone can be the same on the inside with the love and life of Jesus dwelling inside them. Beauty only comes from the heart; a pretty smile is just an added bonus.

Women desire beauty because they think it provides security, a sense of worthiness, popularity, affection, attention, and position. But in fact, outward beauty only provides these things in a temporary state. Beauty will fade, attention will fade, fame will fade, fortune will fade, positions will fade, but the true beauty of Jesus will live forever. His beauty will never fade, and is always permanently fixed. Nancy Friday, writer of beauty writes, "None of us escapes the influence that our looks have had on our lives. Beauty has become what our lives are about, not the clothes and seasonable fashions, but the rage, grief, a terrible sense of isolation that we get when we don't get back any good feeling from the money and time we invest in appearance." People go to great lengths to look and feel beautiful, just to have those efforts go in vain. True beauty cannot be found in temporary things, but can only be found through eternal things. The mirror, like one's beauty, will one day grow dim and fade away. Don't put your worth in your beauty because your beauty will never be worth it. Jesus is the only eternal mirror that reflects true everlasting and brilliant beauty.

Beauty is in the eye of the beholder and that eye is of God. Every woman that God has created is beautiful to him. He took the time to create each one the way he wanted them to be. We are created in his image[2] and God is beautiful. What God sees and what man sees are two different things. God does not see as man sees. The Bible tells us that "God does not look at the appearance or at the physical stature, for the Lord does not see as man sees for man looks at the outward appearance, but the Lord looks at the heart," (I Samuel 16:7).

We can see from these scriptures the man looks upon the outward appearance and delights in the pleasure of its sight. God looks upon the inward beauty of the heart and delights in the pleasure of its sight. True beauty is a heart condition. Although we may want to have all the beautiful features of a super model or of a movie star, we should desire the more important features of beauty, a spotless, clean heart that is delightful in the sight of God.

It's okay for a woman to look beautiful and adorn herself with beautiful things, but it isn't okay to place all her identity just in her outward appearance. A person's outward appearance will be noticed by others, but it will be their character that will be remembered the most. Instead let it be of the beautiful colors that radiate from the inside. Your total appearance is all important to God, from the crown of your head, to the tip of your toes, and down to your heart. We are all temples of the Holy Spirit[3] inside and out. We all have an inward man that should look beautiful all the time. Don't practice the ways of the world and only judge someone from the way they look on the outside, but follow God's ways and look into the inward beauty of the heart. If you look into the beauty of one's heart instead of the beauty of one's skin, you may discover a beautiful person underneath that you hadn't noticed before.

Beauty is more than skin deep it is a heart condition. If your heart is glowing and beautiful on the inside, then your face, your attitude, your behavior, your actions, your words, and your appearance will show it. How can I get this beautiful, glowing heart? Two simple solutions to perfect looking skin and a beautiful you: (1) by confessing Jesus as Lord of your life and (2) seeing yourself as God sees you. In God's eyes, you are special, you are good, and you are beautiful. When you look into the mirror, who do you see? Do you see yourself as God sees you? Or, do you see only what the reflection gives back? The main ingredient in this combination solution is letting God into your heart and allowing him to fill you with his beauty. There is only one perfect and beautiful creation: the author, the maker, and the creator of beauty himself, Jesus Christ.

When you accept Jesus as your Lord and Savior, he forgives you of your sins and makes you beautiful on the inside. Upon accepting him into your life, you become a reflection of him, his love, his ways, and his beauty. Your outward beauty is fading each day but it is the inward beauty of the heart that will live forever.

God has created you, and he made you beautiful and special. You are a child of God and have inherited his traits, and guess what? God is beautiful, and that makes you beautiful! It does not matter if you see crooked teeth or frizzy hair. It doesn't matter what someone in your past or present has said, or is saying about you. What matters is this: you are the righteousness of God in Christ Jesus, you are a blood-bought child of God, and you are destined for greatness! Do not let your past shadow your future, and do not let the reflection in the mirror keep you from achieving your destiny. Choose to change the colors in your make-up bag and replace them with the colors of salvation, joy, happiness, and forgiveness. Your face and your heart will thank you.

I Timothy 4:4 says everything God created is good. You are good, you are beautiful, and you are not a mistake. God has chosen you from many.[4] Recognize who you are, stand up, and be the beauty you really are! If you have been blessed with outward beauty but don't have the beauty of Christ on the inside, what good is that beauty? Your outward beauty will one day pass away, but the beauty of a heart filled with Jesus will live forever with him in eternity. You are a true divine design; let your beauty shine. Take the time to look at yourself in the mirror and hold your head up high, confess aloud to yourself, "I am special!" "I am chosen!" "I am beautiful!" "I am a king's daughter a princess by appointment."

 **Princess Bible Verse:**

Proverbs 31:30

"Charm is deceptive, and beauty is vain (because it is not lasting), but a woman who reverently and worshipfully fears the Lord, she shall be praised."

Princess Prayer:

Lord, I thank you that you have given me everything I need to accomplish what you have set before me to do. I pray that you will continually open the eyes of my understanding to recognize the potential you have placed inside me. I thank you that you have a plan for my life and you have given me the beauty of your son Jesus. I pray for your help each day to see myself beautiful, special, and talented. I pray that you will help me to see your perfect beauty reflecting in the mirror and not the flaws of my natural skin. In Jesus' name, Amen.

 Princess Beauty Tips:

A princess's heart should be the picture of true beauty. Use the picture to answer the following questions. How much of your heart is filled with the love of Jesus? How much is filled with your own desires and ambitions? Do you have anger, bitterness, and unforgiveness in your heart?

 *Princess Confessions:*

I am a princess a member of the royal family of Jesus Christ. I will use my beauty, grace, and poise for the glory of God.

 Princess Challenge:

Make a daily decision to look more into the mirror of God's word to enhance your beauty and less into the mirror on the wall.

 Princess Crown Thought:

Worldly beauty is only skin deep, but the love and beauty of God will make you complete.

Mirror, mirror on the wall, who's the fairest one of all?

It is the one who lives within, my very own and precious skin.

I'm bought and paid for with a price, the living God named Jesus Christ,

Shed his blood so I could live, with beauty, grace, and joy within.

By: L Harris

Princess Journaling Assignment:

How many times do you look into the mirror? What do you see? How often do you read and study God's word? What's in your heart reflects your face. *As in water face reflects face, So a man's heart reveals the man. Proverbs 27:19* What's in your heart?

_____
_____
_____
_____
_____
_____
_____
_____
_____
_____
_____
_____
_____
_____
_____
_____

Write Your Own Prayer:

Chapter 4

God and Your Body

Your body is important to God and God needs your body as a vessel to spread the gospel of Jesus Christ. In the Bible, our body is referred to as a holy temple. The very place where the Holy Spirit dwells. I Corinthians 6:19 (NIV) tells us, "Do you not know that your body is a temple of the Holy Spirit, who is in you, whom you have received from God? You are not your own; you were bought at a price. Therefore honor God with your body."

This scripture explains that once we have accepted Jesus as our Lord and Savior, we are no longer our own. God himself uses our body as a dwelling place for his spirit making our body sacred, holy ground. If our body is a temple for the Lord to dwell, we should be proud of it and keep it clean, well groomed, and in good shape. Our temple, or body, should be cleaned and maintained daily, inside and out. As a princess, your body is important to God. Without your body, how would he accomplish his purpose and see his glory in the earth? God needs your hands, your feet, and every part of you in order to help carry out his perfect plan. How would you feel if you walked into your church building and noticed the wallpaper coming down, light bulbs burned out, the floor dirty, and everything dusty? You would think the person in charge did not care much about the building and taking good care of it. That is how it is with your body. When others see you, what do they see? Do they see someone that is well maintained, or someone who is falling apart inside and out?

God invested time, love, and creativity into creating you. Shouldn't you love and invest time in taking good care of his creativity? You were knitted in the thoughts of God and then placed into the womb of your mother. God has given you your own genetic code, your own unique fingerprints, your own personality, and your own voiceprint. You have the fingerprints of Christ all over you.

Do not abuse your temple by painting it with tattoos, piercing it with all kinds of jewelry, or just feeding it junk food. You will not go to hell for painting it or piercing it, but acknowledge him before you do something to your body and he will direct your paths. Don't do something that you may regret later in life. Love you and your body.

Your feelings about your body are intertwined with the feelings you have about yourself. If you don't like whom you are or the way you look, your appearance will reflect those feelings. If you are full of confidence and like whom you are, then your appearance will reflect that as well.

When taking good care of yourself consider your entire body inside and out. All parts of you are important. Your spirit like your body needs three healthy meals a day, and by feeding it the word of God it will stay healthy.

Your spirit not only needs to be fed every day, but it also needs to be cleansed. Cleanse your spirit by repenting of your sins and allowing the blood of Jesus to wash them away. Isaiah 1:16 says, "Wash yourselves, make yourselves clean; put away the evil of your doings from before my eyes! Cease to do evil." God sees and cares about all of you. That is why it is important to maintain both body and spirit. Your spirit will live forever. You choose where it will live. God created you to live in heaven eternally with him. He created Hell only for the devil and the fallen angels.

How can you keep your spirit strong? In some ways, it is very simple, but in others, it will take time, dedication, and faithfulness. First, feed your spirit man the word of God on a daily basis. Just like your body needs food and water to stay healthy, so does your spirit. The word of God is food for the spirit. How will you keep in good shape spiritually and grow more in the Lord, if you do not eat and drink of his word?

Second, pay attention to what you are taking into your spirit through your ears and through your eyes, both of these are gateways to your soul. Don't feed your spirit man junk food by watching rated R movies or TV shows that are full of bad language, sex scenes, nudity, or evilness. Don't just let anything and everything enter into your eyes and ears; protect your spirit and soul by keeping a close guard on them.

The Bible tells us to keep our foot from evil and live unto righteousness. It doesn't matter if your friends are watching it or listening to it, don't let yourself become a garbage can. Make the decision to be set apart from the world.

Now let's talk about the outward body again. Beauty is more than applying make-up, bathing, grooming your hair, and putting on beautiful clothes. Beauty comes from the inside, and taking care of you plays an important role on how you look and feel.

Your body will not shape-up by itself or stay clean all the time, you will have to take care of it. It will never be perfect, no matter how hard you try to make it perfect. You will not be made perfect until the day your body is glorified in Jesus. However, you can strive for a close resemblance of perfection by taking pride in the way you look.

You have to sand down an old, rough piece of wood, trim it down, and paint it to improve its appearance.[1] The same goes for your body. You have to sand down some rough edges, clean it up, apply some paint where needed, and trim off a little in order for it to look its best.

You can use the most expensive make-ups, shampoos, and nail polishes to improve the way you look, but if you do not feel good on the inside, it will not show on the outside. You have to take care of your body before it will take care of you. Do not forget you have been created wonderfully and fearfully in the image of God. Take care of what God has worked hard to create.

How to Care for Your Body

A woman should bathe at least once a day to keep her body looking beautiful, clean, and smelling fresh. Proper cleansing is the most important thing you can do for yourself. A clean, fresh smelling body is more appealing than a quart of the most expensive perfume.

Bathing is simply a combination of water, soap, and a little bit of scrubbing to remove the de-beautifiers (dirt, oil, perspiration) that settle onto your body. Try these helpful hints for getting the most out of each bath. Make sure that your bath or shower water is warm and not hot. Although a very hot bath or shower may feel good, hot water tends to rob your skin of its natural oils and can cause dry and flaky skin if the moisture is not replaced. Once in the tub or shower, don't forget to use that bar of soap in the soap dish. Use it to work up a good rich lather on a sponge or washcloth.

Use soaps with moisturizers or an anti-bacterial formula; any soap is better than none. Lather yourself well all over. Use a long handled brush for those hard to reach places. Don't be afraid to scrub. Brisk scrubbing stimulates circulation and loosens embedded oil and dirt. Scrub your fingernails, elbows, toes, heels, and the soles of your feet with a stiff brush or a gentle abrasive soap. This will remove the dirt and grime from those places that are harder to get clean.

Now that you have properly cleansed your body, rinse well with warm water. Dry yourself well to prevent your skin from chapping. After drying is a great time to apply lotions to your hands, feet, elbows, and legs, or for pushing back fingernail cuticles.

If your hands and feet are severely dry and chapped, apply a thick layer of moisturizing lotion and cover them while your sleep. You can use a pair of lightweight cotton gloves for your hands and a lightweight cotton sock for your feet. Doing so will help restore the moisture back into your skin. After your bathing regimen, take the time to groom yourself with products that will help keep you feeling fresh all day.

Products like deodorant and perfumes can help keep you smelling fresh. Remember when using perfumes, fragrance lotions, or sprays, less is more. Do not over-power yourself and others with smelly ups. Applying a small drop of liquid perfume on the inside of your wrist or behind one ear will be sufficient. When using a spray perfume, spray fragrance in front of you and walk through it. This will help you from applying too much at one time.

The rule is…if you can smell yourself, it is probably enough. Although smelling pretty is an advantage, too many combinations of fragrances can distract and take away from your over-all appearance. Always use your fragrance choice in moderation. You can look beautiful and be dressed to the "T" but if you reek with perfume or even body odor, who will notice? There is no need to apply perfumes and deodorants before bedtime, give your body and others around you the chance to breath.

Shaving Tips

Women haven't always shaved their legs. Shaving became popular during World War II when women could not buy nylons to cover their legs. It was against the law to buy nylons during this time. Nylon was used to make supplies for the war. Nylons were in short supply, and women had to learn to take care of them before they became too damaged to wear. Women would go to great lengths to cover their legs. If their stockings were torn, they simply went to a seamstress who could sew them up, or they did the repair themselves. If the stockings were too torn to wear, women would paint their legs just to camouflage them. Because of the short supply of nylon stockings during the war, bare legs became a trend that has continued until this day.

There are many ways to remove unwanted hair from your legs and underarms. The most common technique involves using a razor. Some women prefer using wax or "wipe on" and "wipe off" hair removal products. However, these techniques are painful and stinky. Whatever technique you decide to use, make sure you understand what you are doing before you actually do it.

To shave under your arms or on your legs, you must first wet them with warm water and lather with soap or shaving cream. The heat and moisture will help ease the hair removing process. Don't shave legs when they are dry. This is painful and causes your skin to become very dry. Your legs have few oil glands to help keep them soft. Apply a generous amount of soap or shaving cream to your legs. Since the hairs on your legs grow down, you will want to start from the ankle and work your way up. For your underarms you will have to shave in many directions. There is no need to use expensive shaving creams; most of them are the same. Using a simple bar of soap will lather just as well.

When choosing a razor, choose one with a pivot head and multiple blades to help in removing hair. Experiment and find out which one works best for you. Never leave your razor blade exposed to water. Keep it covered, clean, and dry to avoid blades from rusting. Never shave with a rusty razor, and change it at the first sight of dullness or rusting.

Try exfoliating your legs with a sugar and water paste to soften up skin and remove dead skin cells before starting to shave. Exfoliating your skin will also help with any problems due to ingrown hairs. Shave carefully around your ankles and knees. This area is very easy to nick. Instead of shaving with your leg bent at the knee, keep your leg out straight. You can shave up past your kneecap, or you can shave all the way up to your panty line; either way is right.

After you have shaved the unwanted hair from your legs, apply a generous amount of skin cream to help restore moisture. There is no need to put lotion under your arms, only deodorant should be placed there.

Princess Bible Verse

Psalm 139:14 NKJV

"I will praise you, for I am fearfully and wonderfully made, marvelous are your works, and that my soul knows very well."

Princess Grooming Evaluation

Do I take a bath daily?	Always	Sometimes	Never
Do I wash my hair at least every other day?	Always	Sometimes	Never
Do I keep my ears cleaned out regularly?	Always	Sometimes	Never
Do I take good care of my skin?	Always	Sometimes	Never
Do I wash my face in the morning and at night?	Always	Sometimes	Never
Do I use deodorant?	Always	Sometimes	Never
Do I brush my teeth at least twice a day?	Always	Sometimes	Never
Do I go to bed with make-up on my face?	Always	Sometimes	Never
Do I change my clothes every day?	Always	Sometimes	Never
Do I comb and brush my hair?	Always	Sometimes	Never

What can I do to take better care of myself?

_____

_____

_____

_____

Princess Beauty Tips

A bar of soap is a beauty product that a princess should use to wash away the dirt and grime from her body. A bar of soap can be compared to the blood of Jesus. Jesus died on the cross and shed his blood to wash away your sins. His blood will wash away the dirt and grime of sin from your life.

Princess Confessions

I am fearfully and wonderfully made. I have been created in the image of God.

Princess Prayer

Lord, help me to love and respect my body and to be thankful for it. Help me to resist temptations and to make wise choices. I take authority over my body and declare that sickness and disease shall not enter my dwelling, no evil shall befall me, and obesity and sloppiness has no place in my life. Give me a strong desire to stay in shape body, soul, and spirit. In Jesus' name, Amen.

Princess Challenge

Evaluate your eating habits and exercise schedule. Try to invest more time in taking care of your body and be diligent in doing so.

Princess Crown Thought

Take pride in your body and how you take care of it. God has fearfully and wonderfully created you.[2] Wonderfully means you are distinctively unique. You are a one of a kind masterpiece.

Princess Journaling Assignment:

Am I taking good care of my body? Am I doing all I can to stay in shape spiritually, mentally, and physically? What are some things I can do to improve my life?

_____
_____
_____
_____
_____
_____
_____
_____
_____
_____
_____
_____
_____
_____
_____
_____
_____
_____

Write Your Own Prayer:

Chapter 5

God and Exercise

Keeping your body physically fit is important. Getting the right amount of exercise and eating the right kinds of food each day will help you stay on the right track. Let's say you have been eating nothing but junk food, and getting no exercise; do you think this will help you stay physically fit? Of course, the answer to that question would be no. Watching the foods you eat and exercising will help you stay physically fit. A little exercise every day, no matter what kind, is always good for your body. Sitting in front of the television or lying around listening to the radio, will not benefit you.

God made your body to be on the move. Think about it; everything on the inside and on the outside of you is constantly moving. So use your body the way God intended it to be used. Shake off that laziness, pull yourself up off that couch, throw out the junk food, and get to moving. Make a difference for your body's sake. Proverbs 19:15 in the New Kings James Version reads, "Laziness casts one into a deep sleep, and an idle person will suffer hunger."

Everyone can find some way or sometime to exercise. Walking, jogging, horseback riding, swimming, bicycling, or any other type of physical activity can be added to your daily routine. With a little bit of dedication and perseverance you can have the body you so desire. Finding time in your schedule to exercise is a good start in getting your body into shape. Only twenty minutes of moderate exercise a day can enhance your energy level, increase your metabolism, increase blood flow, strengthen your heart, burn fat, and help your mind and body stay healthy. You will feel happier and look great. Remember: Diet affects your weight, and exercise affects your shape, and neither can do the job for the other, although they do work hand in hand.

God made women in all different shapes and sizes. Don't waste your time worrying over how tall or short you are. You cannot add inches to your height or shed pounds by worrying about it. If you have a problem with your height or weight, ask the Lord to help you find peace with the way he has made you to be. One thing is for certain, you cannot change the genetics of how you are shaped or how tall you are. Those two things will most likely stay the same once you have reached adulthood.

You do have the power to change your body with a little bit of dedication, self-control, and hard work. If you are a bit over-or-under weight, you can make a difference through proper nutrition and plenty of exercise. You have to put your mind to it before your body will do it.

Women are naturally fluffy in some areas, and when you have children you will understand why. The problem starts when we let our bodies become overly fluffy. If you are a little fluffy and you would like to get into shape, or would simply like to improve your muscle tone, join a fitness or walking club, hire a personal trainer or surf the web for daily exercises you can do to help you stay in shape and work troubled areas.

Your Weight

Determine your ideal weight by consulting your doctor or reading literature that will give you some ideas on the weight you should be according to your frame size. Remember, the idea is to achieve a healthy weight. An unrealistic size would be 6' tall and one hundred pounds. How do you determine an ideal weight for yourself? Weight does not always follow some tidy and neat equation. Instead of asking yourself, "What is an ideal weight?" Ask yourself, "What is a healthful and achievable weight for me?" Many believe that focusing on how to develop a healthful lifestyle that would include good foods and plenty of physical activity is more important than achieving an ideal weight.

A healthy body weight should be one that you can maintain with some vigilance, but one that will not severely limit your food intake. Eating living, healthy foods can improve your overall physique. Living foods include fresh or cooked fruits and vegetables, and whole grain products. Only you can determine your weight gain or your weight loss. Get to know your body and the foods that will help you maintain your ideal weight. For some, losing weight and breaking themselves from old habits will be hard. You have to be dedicated to living a healthy lifestyle. It is not something that will happen overnight. It will take time and patience. Avoid crazy diets.

Losing and regaining weight is not healthy for your body and you may end up in worse shape than you started. If you need to lose weight, start by losing five to ten percent of your total weight, and then modify your lifestyle to maintain it. Try adding more physical activity to your lifestyle and eliminating those extra calories from your diet. Eat wisely, and decrease your sugar intake by drinking less sugared drinks and eating less junk food. Another way to help you lose weight is by simply consuming smaller portions.

You should never lose more than one to two pounds a week. Losing weight can improve your health, but if not done properly it can also be hazardous to your health. Setting an unrealistic weight to achieve can lead to eating disorders such as anorexia or bulimia. Think smart and ask your doctor what realistic weight loss plan would be easiest and best for you to achieve.

Princess Bible Verse

Proverbs 10:4 "He becomes poor who works with a slack and idle hand, but the hand of the diligent makes rich."

Princess Beauty Tips

Weights are tools a princess can use to get into shape. When they are used repeatedly and on a regular basis, they can help strengthen muscles. The Bible is much like a weight. When read and used on a regular basis, it will help you stay in shape and strengthen your faith muscles.

Princess Confessions

My body is a temple where the spirit of God lives and dwells. I confess to take care of it to the best of my ability.

Princess Prayer

Lord, I ask for your strength to help me keep my body in shape and eat only those things which are good for me. I understand that my body is not my own and that it belongs to you. I thank you Lord for your strength to resist temptations when dealing with food. Teach me how to eat and do what is best all the time so I will always be in good health and in good shape. In Jesus' name, Amen.

Princess Challenge

Make an extra effort to get more exercise, eat more salad, and drink less soda.

Princess Crown Thought

Your body is the temple of the Holy Spirit; make it a place he will be proud to dwell.

Princess Journaling Assignment:

Are you getting enough exercise each day? Make a list of the ways you are getting exercise and make a plan to add more if needed. Are you being a good steward of your body? Are you striving for the spirit of excellence in all areas of your life. Why, or why not?

Write Your Own Prayer:

Chapter 6

God and Your Skin

Your skin is the largest organ of your body containing 6 percent of your body weight, 33 percent of your blood, and is made up of 70 percent water. The skin acts like wrapping paper for your bones, muscles, and tissue. The skin also acts as a waist disposer for water and mineral wastes, a manufacturer of oil, and a base for hair follicles (a hair follicle is a single depression in the scalp and skin out of which a single hair grows). The skin is a shelter for nerves, blood vessels, sebaceous glands, and sweat glands. Sebaceous glands secrete a fatty or oily substance, a regulator for body temperature, and a protector from bacteria and body dehydration. The face has more sebaceous glands, mostly located on the forehead, nose, and chin areas. This area is usually described by dermatologist as the "T" zone.

The skin is made up of two layers: (1) the epidermis, or visible, outer layer which you see and (2) the dermis, or inner, layer underneath the epidermis. The sweat glands, sebaceous (oil) glands, hair follicles, nerve endings, and blood vessels are located in the dermis. The skin on your face is more delicate than the skin on the rest of your body and needs special cleansing regimens to keep it healthy and glowing. Although all your skin is important, the skin on your face is usually what people notice first. Your skin tells a lot about who you are, and speaks to others by the way it looks.

Skin comes in many colors. In the beginning, when God created man and woman, we are not told what color of skin they had; and it really doesn't matter. They were made in the image of God, and God's skin color is beautiful. No matter if you were born black, white, red, or yellow, it is all beautiful in God's eyes. Your skin color, thickness, and oiliness are inherited features. Skin does change with age, climate, and exposure to sun and wind. However, like your personality, your skin is your own. You have the power to determine the appearance and beauty of your skin by the way you choose to care for it. Take care of your skin and protect it. It is never too late to start a daily facial regimen.

As early as eight years old, you should be aware of the importance of keeping your childlike complexion. Start caring for your skin now, so that it will look young when you are older. Between the ages of twelve and sixteen, you may start having problems with your skin. It is at this time your body chemistry starts working against you leaving your skin "confused." During this confusing state, keep up with your daily facial cleansing routine and avoid letting it get the best of you. When you reach seventeen to eighteen years old, your complexion starts to harmonize with your body chemistry and any skin problems start to let up. There are many ways to treat troubled skin, and understanding your skin type will help you care for it properly. It is not hard to have great looking skin if you discipline yourself and invest the time.

To care for your skin, it is important you recognize your individual skin type. Everyone's skin is made-up differently, so what works for your friend may not work for you. Skin types are divided into four groups: normal, dry, oily, and combination. Use this simple test to determine your skin type. Early in the morning, before washing your face, take a white tissue paper (ex. tissue gift wrap paper), or a brown paper bag, cut four, one-half strips about two inches long, and press a strip lightly on your forehead, chin, nose, and cheek. Labeling the papers will help you determine your troubled spots. If the tissue or paper sticks to your face and shows no oily patches, your skin type is normal. If the tissue sticks readily, and oily patches show up on the paper, your skin type is oily. If the tissue barely sticks or falls off, your skin type is dry. When you have determined your skin type, you can then refer to the following information on how to care for it.

Skin Types

Normal skin is durable, soft, glowing, and requires the least amount of care. It has a firm, smooth texture that springs back when pinched. Pores are almost invisible. To cleanse normal skin, use a mild soap and lukewarm water each morning and evening. Work up a good lather and gently massage your skin with your fingertips. Be sure to cleanse your neck; it is also part of your face. Rinse with warm water and then pat your skin dry with a clean towel. Apply a moisturizer at the first sign of dryness. Once a week, use an exfoliating product to remove dead skin cells and keep the pores clean. A wet washcloth rubbed over the face and body can be used to exfoliate without having to use any products.

Dry skin feels tight after washing with soap and water. It chaps and flakes easily, and is accompanied by fine lines appearing all too early. Use a washable cream to cleanse. Rinse off thoroughly with water. Use an exfoliating product once a week to remove dead cells. Having a well-balanced diet and drinking lots of water daily will help hydrate dry skin and keep it looking beautiful. Avoid using astringents and medicated cosmetics or soaps. Using an avocado facemask will help restore natural oils.

Oily skin tends to have a coarse texture, feels sticky, and is prone to blemishes, blackheads, and enlarged pores. Wash as often as you can. Spend at least five minutes each morning and evening cleansing your face. Use a mild drying agent, such as an astringent, to help tighten your pores. Use an exfoliating product to remove dead cells. Gently rubbing your face with ground up almonds and honey made into a paste will help reduce blackheads and open up clogged pores. Make sure you are eating fresh fruits and vegetable high in antioxidants. Drink lots of water to increase the circulation and help move unwanted toxins from your body. Stay away from creamy cleansers and heavy, pore-clogging make-up. Be sure to use a water-based instead of an oil-based make-up. Try applying foundation make-up only to uneven skin tone areas instead of covering your entire face. Instead of using a powder to reduce shine, keep a clean tissue on hand to blot excess oil. Let your skin breath at night. To help absorb extra oils in the skin, use a clay mask once a week. Clay is an absorbent and tightens pores. Clay masks date back to the days of Cleopatra.

Combination skin is firm, smooth in texture, and has an oily and dry zone. The dry areas are usually around your eyes, on your cheeks and jaw line. The oily zone or the "T" zone is found on the forehead, around the nose, and chin. To treat combination skin, simply wash with a mild soap, paying attention to your "T" zone area. Using an avocado mask or a clay mask once a week will help reduce the oily and dry areas and will help bring balance. Only apply the avocado mask to the dry areas of your face and the clay mask to the oily parts.

All skin needs toning. Toning lotions help make the skin look firm, poreless, and smooth. Toning lotions should be applied to the skin after it has been washed and dried. They are available in two types; skin fresheners and astringents. A skin freshener is made of alcohol and various additives. They make the skin feel cool and refreshed. They remove both grease from oily skin and the sticky residue of washable creams. An astringent contains mostly water and small amounts of alcohol and aluminum salts. They have a special ability to make big pores seem smaller. If skin gets dry or irritated using this product, use a milder astringent. Lime or lemon extract gives the toner a balanced pH - an important quality for acne skin. Use caution when using a freshener or astringent, as they can cause a sharp stinging sensation to your skin. If the sensation is too strong for you, try using a milder product made for sensitive skin. Use an astringent or toner on oily skin types or in the combination "T" zone area. Dry skin already has naturally tight pores and can be aggravated by an astringent.

Cleansing and toning leaves pores wide open. A light moisturizer is required to help cover and protect open pores. Lanolin, which is very similar to body oil, is usually the main ingredient in moisturizer creams. If you have oily skin, use moisturizers sparingly. Oil on top of oil is not good. If you have combination skin, apply moisturizer only to dry areas. Remember to let your face breathe at night no matter what type of skin you may have. Make it a rule: no products at bedtime.

Knowing your skin type and how to care for it will not be enough to help keep skin looking healthy. There are also many other factors to consider. For example, eight hours of sleep, eating healthy foods, exercising, living a stress-free life, and drinking lots of water will help aid in great looking skin. To determine the amount of water you need a day, take your weight and divide it by two, for example (114lbs = 57 oz). Water helps eliminate impurities from your body, keeps your skin and body hydrated, helps burn calories, and fills your stomach so you do not want to eat as much. If you can't get your daily recommended allowance of water a day, try drinking as much as you can. Start slowly and work your way up. An adult needs at least one quart of water a day to remain healthy. Water is the least expensive yet the most important thing you can do for your skin. Eating healthy foods and three balanced meals a day will also play an important role on the way your skin looks. Include in your diet a combination of meats, leafy greens, yellow vegetables, fruits, dairy products, breads, and cereals. Milk, basmati rice, almonds, and oranges help give the skin a healthy glow. Your skin needs important vitamins only found in fruits and vegetables. Avoid eating and drinking foods that are high in sugar, like chocolate, candies, teas, and soda pop. Carbonated drinks rob oxygen from your body's system and the decrease of oxygen in your body results in sluggish circulation. A little sugar is okay, but you can overload your system with too much sugar. This can cause unwanted pimples and acne problems in some people.

Getting eight hours of sleep each night will benefit your skin in a tremendous way. Sleep replenishes your system and helps your body repair itself from the day's wear and tear. Sleep will help your skin look refreshed and full of life. Never neglect your body the proper amount of sleep it needs each day. Pay attention as to what your body is telling you and respond accordingly. Living a stress-free life is hard to do but it can be accomplished. Choose to remove as much stress as possible. Stress not only causes skin problems, but it can also affect your overall health.

Not only are there many skin types, but there are also many types of skin problems. Some women are blessed with problem free skin and others have to work at keeping their complexion looking healthy and glowing. The most common blemishes are blackheads and pimples. Blackheads are small masses of dead cells, oil, and bacteria that collect in the pore openings and trap dirt on top. Blackheads are simply just plugs of dirt in your pores. Use warm water and a rough washcloth, briskly and thoroughly wash

your skin. For those stubborn blackheads, cleanse with a grainy cleanser or blackhead treatment. A paste made from sugar and water works well. There is no need to spend a lot of money on purchasing blackhead treatments when the best exfoliators are right in your kitchen or already in your bathroom. Although squeezing is the only way to remove stubborn blackheads, don't attempt to remove them without first knowing how to do it properly. A moist face makes it easier to remove unwanted blackheads. After taking a hot steaming bath or shower is a great time to operate.

Don't remove blackheads forcefully, as doing so can result in enlarged pores and can also cause permanent scaring. Use the pads of your fingertips and gently push to dislodge the blackheads. Your face will be red for a short time but the color will quickly fade back to normal.

Everyone has occasional pimples. Pimples are just blackheads enlarged and inflamed. The bacteria and dirt trapped inside your pore causes a reaction and a pimple forms. Simply wash your face with soap and water and stick to your daily facial routine to avoid these kinds of flare-ups. Apply a greaseless, flesh-tinted medicated cream or lotion to help camouflage pimples while they are healing. Do not attempt to hide your blemishes with a thick, oil-based make-up; always use a water base make-up. Do not pick, squeeze, or even touch pimples any more than you have to. The best solution is to keep your hands off, allow your skin to breath, and let it heal on its own.

Gently washing your face with a grainy facial cleanser like the sugar/water mixture mentioned for blackhead removal, can be very effective in helping eliminate the reoccurrence of pimples. In the early 1700's, a common beauty regimen for treating pimples included eating cucumbers, mixed with oatmeal and mutton, for three weeks. This wasn't the only treatment required. The patient also had to wash his or her face with a mixture of vinegar, orrice roots, brimstone, camphor, almonds, apples, and lemon juice! Aren't you glad for advanced technology and beauty treatments?

Another popular way to treat pimples in the 1700's was to camouflage them with decorative stickers called beauty patches. They would cut out decorative shapes and different sizes and glue them to their face wherever the blemish was to be found. Can you image your face one big sticker on your worst blemished day?

Acne is another type of skin problem. Sometimes inflamed pimples do not clear-up but rather go deeper into the skin, destroying tissue and creating permanent pits and scars. Severe acne needs special attention; it will not go away by itself. Cleanse your skin at least three times a day and keep your hair clean as well. Troubled skin usually finds company with an oily scalp.

Watch your diet and eat foods that are helpful to your skin instead of harmful. Stay away from greasy foods, chocolate, spicy dishes, and drink plenty of water each day. Your skin is often referred to as the third kidney, and when a kidney is in distress it lets your body know by reacting accordingly. When a person has a skin issue, most likely there is an internal source not in perfect balance. Keep your hands off your face and always remember that with man it is impossible, but with God all things are possible (Matthew 19:26).

Zit Zappers

- Shrink swelling of infected blemishes with an ice pack.

- Apply a drop of eye drops to the blemish to reduce the redness.

- Mix dry yeast and water to form a paste. Apply mixture to the affected area, let dry, and wash off in the morning.

- Don't squeeze your blemishes. Squeezing causes enlarged pores. If you have to squeeze, use the pads of your fingers and don't use your nails.

Freckles

Freckles or sunspots and moles are as common as peanut butter and jelly. Almost everyone has freckles somewhere on their body. They appear in different shapes and sizes and some are uniquely placed. They can become a trademark to your appearance. They are a part of you and God gave them to you. Don't ever be ashamed or embarrassed by them. If you have a mole in a place that becomes troublesome, you can have them burned off by your doctor or dermatologist. Freckles on the other hand will have to stay but can be evened out by using a flesh tone liquid make-up or concealer.

In early historical times, it was not fashionable for a woman to have freckles, birthmarks, or any other kind of blemish on her face. In fact, the more fair or pale skinned the lady appeared, the more socially acceptable she was in her community. Women would go to great lengths to get rid of freckles or marks of any kind. They would even go as far as washing their face with a potion that included mercury. Mercury is a chemical that can burn the top layer of skin completely off and everything else in its way. To think someone would go to the length of risking her own life just to get rid of a freckle or birthmark is astonishing!

Unwanted Hair

Unwanted facial hair can be both bothersome and unattractive. Dark facial hair is found most commonly above the upper lip and can be easily removed with hot wax. If you have unwanted hair anywhere on your face, don't shave it off! This will only encourage thicker and more noticeable hair to start growing back. The best solution is to ask your beautician about facial waxing to avoid any mistakes.

Factors that can Affect Your Skin

- Keep your hands off your face. Allowing your hands to touch your face at night or during the day is not a good thing. Your hands house oils and bacteria--oil and bacteria cause problems for your skin. Make it a habit to wash your hands regularly. In addition, the constant folding on the skin can cause unwanted wrinkles.

- Never go to bed with make-up on your face. Stay on schedule with your facial cleansing routine. Your skin collects grit and grime throughout the day and it settles into your pores. Even though you may not see dirt, there is hidden dirt that needs to be removed. Always wash your face.

- Stay out of the sun as much as possible and avoid tanning beds. The sun dries out the skin. Wear protective covering and lotions when you have to be in the direct sunlight. For example, a white t-shirt only provides a SPF of eight. Cover-up as much skin as possible.

- Give your skin a break from wearing make-up or moisturizers. Apply a daily, light moisturizer to your face before applying make-up. Avoid wearing a night cream or moisturizing lotion to bed. Your face is covered with some kind of application at least eight to ten hours a day; let your skin breath for at least that long at night.

- Extreme hot or cold weather conditions can and will cause skin problems if you do not take care of your skin according to the climate in which you live. For example, hot and dry weather can result in dry, itchy, or flaky skin. The key is to keep your skin clean and moisturized to avoid any problems.

- Your body needs good circulation to stay healthy. To help produce good circulation, drink enough water, get enough exercise, practice facial remedies, like massages or applying a cleansing mask.

- Be gentle with your skin, especially the skin on your face and around your eyes. Remember to always apply a minimum amount of pressure and use an upward stroke.

- Some medication can cause skin irritations. If you are taking any medications, make sure you take time to read the side effects, so you will be aware of any problems that could occur.

Smiling creates a beautiful face. It takes ten muscles to smile and seventy to frown. Your face tends to shape to the expression you most usually wear. Wear your smile often and avoid letting your face become stiff. Relax your face muscles by smiling as large as you can and opening your mouth at the same time. Do this several times in a row. Yawn big and stretch your muscles to help relax your face muscles.

Revivers and Relaxers

Read a magazine, read an uplifting article or book, or simply flip through a catalog.

Go to a spa for a massage, manicure, facial, or pedicure.

Catch up on your sleep.

Work in the garden, flower bed, or enjoy some other relaxing hobby.

Read God's word and refresh your mind and spirit.

Watch a clean comedy TV show.

Make yourself laugh.

Live, laugh, love, and go shopping!

Check your posture. Roll your shoulders back and forth and your head side to side.

Eat a piece of fruit when you filled zapped of energy; preferably an orange or banana.

Take deep breaths.

Yawn.

Pray.

Cast your cares and concerns on the Lord.

Take a relaxing bath or shower. Rub your shoulders and legs while you soak.

Drink a glass of water.

Take a ten to fifteen-minute power nap.

Exercise to increase your circulation.

Wrap your arms around you and hug yourself. Rub your shoulder blades while doing so.

Rub your cheekbones and jaw line while opening and closing your mouth.

Safe in the Sun

The color of skin has been an issue all throughout history. In the 1700's, it was not proper to have tanned skin. In fact, the mask was born in this era. Men and women would shade their faces from the sun with masks on sticks with colorful decorations. The more fair skinned a person became the better. They not only carried masks when they walked from place to place, but they also carried them while riding their horses and riding in their buggies. It was also in this time that women and men started washing their faces with skin bleaching substances to achieve a pale white look.

Nowadays, tanning our skin and exposing it to the sun's rays is the social norm. If you are a sun worshiper, protecting your skin from harmful sunrays is vital to your health and should be thoughtfully considered. Protecting your skin means shielding it from the hot sun. As you work at getting a tan, the sun is robbing your skin from its moisture and causing wrinkly, dry skin. The sun damages your skin permanently and is irreversible. Before you go sunbathing or sun bedding, remember what is happening to your skin.

If you insist on the golden bronze look, use a suntan product. The higher the SPF, the longer you can stay in the sun without burning. A product like mineral oil, baby oil, and cocoa butter provide no sun protection and only aids the sun in damaging your skin. Some sun is good for you, so use common sense and avoid over-exposing yourself when possible.

Sun Tips

- Cover your entire body or at least the parts that will be exposed to the sun with a generous amount of water-resistant sunscreen with at least a SPF 15.

- Protect your face with a wide brimmed hat or visor, wear sunglasses with a UV protective lens, and apply extra sunscreen to your nose, ears, and hairline. It is also a good idea to wear a sun blocking lip balm to protect the sensitive skin on your lips.

- Apply sunscreen thirty minutes before going out, giving it time to absorb into your skin. Don't forget to reapply every two hours, especially if you are swimming.

- A spray suntan lotion works well for those hard to reach areas. It is easy to apply and reapply.

- Use caution when you have pale skin. People with a large amount of freckles, light eyes, blonde or red hair tend to burn easily. Make your visits in the sun brief and safe.

- Medications can cause sun irritation and health issues. Always be aware of the products you are taking and the possible side effects of each.

There are many new and exciting self-tanning products on the market. You can find these products in a cream lotion, a spray, a facial powder, and even in a tinted-moisturizer. Why take a chance on permanently damaging your skin from the harmful rays of the sun when you can tan in the privacy of your own home and in a healthy way? If you are set on having that golden bronze look and are considering using a self-bronzing cream or powder, then you must know the right and wrong ways to apply these products.

How to Apply a Self-Tanner

The most important factor in applying a self-tanner is to exfoliate, exfoliate, and exfoliate. Exfoliating your skin simply means rubbing your skin with a rough textured sponge, washrag, or gritty exfoliating substance. By rubbing your skin with a rough surface or substance, you are not only deep cleaning your pores but you are also removing any dead skin cells.

After your skin has been completely exfoliated, you are then able to apply a smooth layer of tanning product, which in return will not look blotchy or rub off easily. An excellent exfoliant is plain white sugar. Put some sugar in a cup or container and add a little bit of water to make a paste then rub it gently onto your face and body. Avoid rubbing too hard so that you don't tear or irritate your skin.

After washing and exfoliating your skin, dry off completely. The one problem most people have with a self-tanning product is the fact that it penetrates deeper in the ankle, kneecap, heel, and elbow areas leaving a darkening effect. The result leaves a fake, painted-on look. The reason this happens is the skin in these areas is tougher and thicker. God made these areas of skin tougher and thicker because he knew we would need extra padding in these areas of our body. To avoid this from happening, apply a small amount of body moisturizer to these areas before applying self-tanner. Let the moisturizer dry completely. The extra moisture creates a barrier and keeps the tanner from penetrating deep into the pores.

It is a good idea wear a pair of disposable latex gloves while you apply your self-lotion. You don't want the tanner to penetrate the skin on the palm of your hands and turn them a yellow color thus, leaving a clue to others that a self-tanner has been used. When applying a tanner to the tops of your hands, do one hand at a time. Let the lotion dry, then re-glove, and do the opposite hand. Always remember to wash your hands thoroughly after completing your tanning process.

Start applying your tanning product to the desired areas you want to be tanned.

Most products are not made for the face, so you will have to buy a tanning product designed for the face or simply exclude tanning your face at all. Start your tanning product from top to bottom. Cover the areas you can reach with ease liberally and ask for assistance to reach those hard to reach areas, like your back. After applying tanner, let the areas you have tanned dry for at least fifteen to twenty minutes before getting dressed.

Once you have applied your self-tanning product and re-applied it often, you should start seeing a change in your skin tone. The keys to a great looking self-tan are to be consistent with re-applying and always make sure you are getting great coverage. Have fun in the sun without stepping outside.

Princess Bible Verse

Psalm 105:4 NIV

"Look to the Lord and his strength; seek his face always."

👑 Princess Beauty Tips

A castle is a place where a princess lives and dwells in safety. It is a place that provides protection and provision. Our skin is the outward covering that is used to protect us from the environment and provides shelter for our inward parts. We could refer to it as our shelter. God has given you a shelter of protection and provision by the blessing he has bestowed on you through the blood of Jesus.

👑 Princess Confessions

I will not be distracted by the imperfections of my skin. My appearance may never be perfect and my skin my never be flawless, but my Jesus loves me no matter what.

👑 Princess Prayer

Lord, thank You for the skin you have placed me in. I realize it is a part of me and I ask for your help to understand how to take care of it properly. I take authority over my skin and confess healthy, glowing, and blemish free skin. In Jesus' name, Amen.

👑 Princess Challenge

Challenge yourself to take better care of your skin and be more diligent with your daily facial routine.

👑 Princess Crown Thought

Laziness and procrastination will rob you of your future and keep you from becoming successful in life.

Princess Journaling Assignment

Explain your skincare routine. Are you doing all that is necessary to maintain great looking skin? Explain how you can do better.

Write Your Own Prayer:

Chapter 7

God and Your Make-up Bag

Many things could be said about God and your make-up bag. Some would say that God is against women wearing make-up, cutting their hair, or wearing fine jewelry and clothes, so let's start by getting one thing straight: God is not against you. Many religions in our world are against women being women, and use the Bible as a weapon against them. One passage of scripture that is often taken out of context is I Peter 3:3-4.

In this passage of scripture, Peter is saying that women should not solely rely on such extremes of adornment of beauty to make them holy or godly, but should only rely on the hidden person of their heart. In Greek, the word "clothes" or "apparel" means garments. If women are not to adorn themselves in garments, then what should they wear, nothing? It's time to start believing the freedom we have in Christ, and respect those freedoms. II Corinthians 3:17 in the New King James Version says, "Now the Lord is the spirit; and where the spirit of the Lord is, there is liberty." If you are a Christian, then you have freedom in Christ Jesus. He died on the cross not only to forgive us of our sins and unrighteousness, but he also did it so we would be free from all bondage.

If a person chooses not to wear make-up because of their belief system, it will not get them any closer to godliness or holiness than someone who does. The only way to true godliness and holiness is the state of one's heart. Having a gentle and quiet spirit is what matters to God the most. It's not about how you choose to wear your hair, make-up, or clothes that will get you close to God, but it is about your relationship. If you are confused about scripture, pray and ask the Lord to give you wisdom and understanding of it. Don't take someone else's word for it; study it for yourself, and only take God's word as the final answer. God's word is always the truth, God created clothes, jewelry, make-up, and other items meant for women to enjoy.

In Genesis, you will discover that God was the first fashion designer when he made garments for Adam and Eve. He is the maker and creator of everything. All things are created under the inspiration and creativity of God. The devil has no creativity in him. He is a thief and a liar. He only takes what God has created and distorts it to his likeness. Princess, don't be deceived. Make-up and nice clothes are meant for you to enjoy. All these things are external things, and we know from reading the Bible that God does not look at external things but he looks at the heart. Your make-up bag should reflect who you are.

If you rely on your make-up bag to work wonders or manifest miracles, you will be disappointed. Only God can work miracles and do the miraculous. Don't put your trust in a tube of red lipstick or bottle of foundation to make you beautiful. True beauty comes straight from the heart of a person, and a tube of lipstick and bottle of foundation is only an added extra to enhance your natural beauty.

Make-up has been around from the beginning of time. Even people in ancient history were known for using cosmetics, both men and women. For example, when the new settlers came from England they met up with the Native Americans. Native Americans were known for their outrageous and creative ways of wearing and making cosmetics. Cosmetics back then were called face and body paints. The new settlers were so intrigued by the style of the Native Americans they adopted some of their customs and made them their own.

Today some customs can still be found. Recipes for homemade beauty regimens, treatments, and cosmetics were very prized possessions back in historical times.

Beauty recipe books were passed down from generation to generation and were studied and practiced very carefully.

Today the way we wear and make cosmetics has changed. Although there are many new ways of making cosmetics, they will never hold a candle to the homemade concoctions of historical times. Ingredients that can be found in cosmetics today are oil and water. Certain other ingredients add color, fragrance, and a longer shelf life. Because cosmetics are alike, there is no relationship between price and satisfaction. Try a variety of products, and choose those that work best for you. Stop using any that cause irritation, itching, or blotches.

Learning to apply cosmetics takes time and practice. The secret to applying make-up successfully, starts with understanding what make-up was meant to be used for. It is not to meant to hide your beauty but rather to enhance it. Using cosmetics, can highlight your natural complexion, enhance your best features, and cover some flaws. It was not meant to create a new face. If used the wrong way, make-up can become artificial and take away from your natural beauty. People will notice the make-up instead of you. God has given everyone natural beauty, and you want to learn how to enhance it and not hide it. Now, let's explore the different types of make-up and how they should be applied.

Foundation Creams

Foundation cream started when the Native American people applied a layer of grease or animal fat onto their skin before they applied their dyes and pigments of color, thus started the use of foundation cream. Foundation creams can be used as your make-up or as a base for blusher and powder. It is meant to add a glow, even out skin tones, and hide small blemishes. It is not meant to change your complexion. Foundation should be matched closely to your natural skin coloring. You do not want to change your skin tone by applying the wrong color. Carefully chosen and correctly applied, it can make your skin appear flawless and add a glow to your skin tone or texture. Most foundations should be applied with a cosmetic wedge or sponge, or foundation brush. You can also use your fingertips, but always make sure they are clean. Not only should your fingertips, wedge, or sponge be clean, your skin should be clean also. Start by placing a dot of foundation to your forehead, cheeks, and chin. Start blending just below the jawline, using an upward stroke and cover your entire face with color. Pay close attention to the hairline, make sure it is well blended to avoid any lines.

Appling make-up in front of a window with natural light will ensure proper blending. If you have that peaches-and-cream complexion, you will not need to use a lot of foundation. If you do not like the feel of foundation all over your face, try applying it to only the areas were skin tone is uneven. Too much foundation can look artificial and cause pores to clog. A great alternative to foundation make-up is a colored pressed or loose powder or mineral powder. If you are under forty years of age, you should reconsider wearing foundation cream at all, and go for a more natural look to wear from day to day. Save your heavy foundation creams for more formal affairs like proms, special pictures, or stage appearances.

Powders

Women and men started using powder in the 1700s when bathing was not the social norm. They did not believe bathing was a healthy thing to practice every day. Therefore, instead of bathing, they drenched themselves with powders, and perfumes to kill the odor of the body. The powder room originated from this practice. One would have a room in their home where they would go to be drenched by their maidservants with a bucket of powder!

Powders are available either as loose powder or in a cake form. They make the skin appear smooth and help prevent shiny skin. Oily skin has a greater need for powder than dry or normal skin does. Loose powder sets the foundation into place. It gives an added glow to your skin. When applying a loose powder, use a cotton ball, powder puff, or a powder brush. By using a powder brush, you can even out and blend the powder into your skin better. Use a powder that compliments your foundation. Do not use a white powder or a color darker than your foundation but instead use one that compliments your foundation. Keep a pressed powder compact on hand for those needed touch-ups during the day.

Eyeliner

The earliest use of eyeliner has been found used by women in Asia and in the Middle East centuries ago. The eyeliner they used was made from a compound called Kohl. Kohl is a chemical preparation used by women to darken the rims of their eyelids and usually consisted of powdered antimony sulphide or lead sulphide.

The way women use eyeliner today has not changed. It is still used to enhance the eye and draw attention to it. Eyeliner is used along the edge of the upper eyelid, right next to the eyelashes, to make the eye appear larger by outlining the shape. Eyeliner can be found in a liquid, gel or pencil. For best results and easier application, a pencil will work the best. The most simple and inexpensive way to apply eyeliner is simply to use what you already have on hand – your eye shadow palette. Use a thin brush that will create a thin line when used. Use your thin line brush, dab it into some water, squeeze the excess, then dab your brush into the color of shadow you would want to use as eyeliner. Simply follow the line of the upper lash with your brush from the inner corner of your eye to the outer corner.

Try to stay as close to the lash line as possible. You can achieve a softer look by smudging the liner or shadow with the end of your pencil, dampened Q-tip, or eyeliner smudger. If you choose to use an eyeliner pencil, make sure it is sharp for a fine line. Eyeliner can be distracting if it is applied incorrectly. Do some experimenting, and find what works best for you. A little liner goes a long way. When lining the lower lash start at the outer corner of your eye and stop half way or just in line with the center of your pupil. Avoid lining your eyes on the inside of your bottom lash, this will make the eyes appear smaller and more narrow.

False Lashes

If you like wearing false lashes, make sure you understand how to apply them to make them appear more natural. First, choose the color, style, and look you want to achieve. Second, if you are wearing a full-length lash, trim to fit the length of your natural lash. Finally, place adhesive on the very edge of the false lash and attach. When attaching, place the lash as close as you can to the base of your upper lash.

It is a good idea to curl your natural lashes before attaching false ones. If you are using individual lash segments, determine the placement of lashes beforehand. You do not have to trim; only glue and use tweezers to help attach in place. Once your false lash is in place, line your upper lid with your favorite eyeliner. False lashes are not meant to be worn on a daily basis. Use good judgment when determining when and where you should wear them.

Mascara

Some women are blessed with long, dark eyelashes and have no need for mascara; but when mascara is applied, it darkens and highlights the eyelashes. For those of us who have lightly colored, thin eyelashes, mascara is the greatest cosmetic ever invented. It also makes the eye appear brighter. It is available in liquid form. To achieve longer and thicker lashes, stroke the mascara on the upper lash, let dry and apply a second coat. Separate any clumps that might have occurred while applying with a brow brush.

If you like to use an eyelash curler, do so with caution. This can be a very dangerous tool. It is very easy to pull out lashes if you are not careful. Make sure your eyelash curler is kept clean and free from dried mascara. It is best to use your curler after your mascara has had time to dry. To achieve a curled look without the use of a curler, simply raise your chin, glance your eyes downward, apply mascara to bottom of your top lash while pulling upward with the applicator at the same time. Several strokes will make your lashes curl naturally. It is not necessary to spend a lot of money on fancy mascaras.

The best mascara is one with a small applicator. A small applicator will help reach all lashes without a lot of mess-up. Finding one that works best for you is most important. For good eye health, your mascara should be changed every three months. Mascara starts to harbor bacteria and can cause eye irritation. The best way to remind yourself to replace your tube is by dating it at time of purchase and taping it to your tube for reminder. If you are having problems with your mascara smudging under your eye, try a new mascara type like a washable waterproof.

Blusher

In the early years of cosmetic history, a woman could not run to the beauty store and buy what she needed to fill her make-up bag. Women had to make most if not all of their cosmetics from home beauty recipes. Blushers, lipsticks, and eye shadows were made mostly from beets. They would soak dyed wool, paper, or felt in a pigment of choice then rub it onto the desired area they wanted to color. All cosmetics should be used to highlight one's natural beauty. A blusher highlights the cheekbone area to give a blushing appearance. Blushers come in cream, stick, powder, and gel form. Choosing the right color of blush that will blend well with your skin tone is important. Wearing the wrong color of blush, not knowing where to place it on your cheek, and wearing it too dark can make all the difference. Apply blusher with a blush brush and never smash the brush next to your skin flattening the bristles. Use easy and light strokes.

Smile in the mirror to determine the apple of your cheek and start applying a light shade. Stroke your brush front to back, apple to hairline. Blend your blusher with a large powder brush. Make sure it is well blended where there are no lines visible. To determine the right color of blush, go for a jog or workout without wearing make-up and the natural blush that appears in your cheeks is a perfect match for your skin tone. This is only one way to determine the right blush color; the best way is to visit a cosmetic counter.

Lips

Lipstick is a girl's best friend; nothing finishes off that perfect look than using a matching lipstick. You can choose from many colors and product types. Lipstick is found in a cream, pencil, or stick, and usually stays on until you wipe it off. To make lipstick last longer, apply foundation to your lips, then lipstick, dust with powder, then reapply color for a second coat. If you are looking for a lipstick that will stick to your lips longer, try using an eight-hour lipstick. It doesn't wear off or come off on anything your lips come in contact with for at least eight hours. To apply, simply follow the natural line of the lip and top with a gloss for that extra shine.

Lip liners can enhance your lipstick color. To apply, simply follow the natural line of the lip before the lipstick color is applied. Like your face, your lips need to be exfoliated and dead cells removed to keep them looking smooth and healthy. To exfoliate your lips, take an old toothbrush and gently brush your lips. Afterward, apply a layer of Vaseline for moisture and shine. This process leaves your lips feeling smooth and subtle.

Eye Shadow

Eye shadow can be found in creams, liquids, powders, pencils, and many beautiful shades. There are many ways to apply eye shadow. Eye shadow when applied correctly can make your eyes look larger and brighter, cause the whites to look whiter, and the colors to look deeper. Just a touch of color will do the trick. Blending is the key. If using more than one color, make sure the colors are blended well.

To achieve perfect looking eye makeup, follow these easy steps. After you have applied your foundation and powder, create a clean palette to apply your eye shadow. To make your eye shadow stay on longer, apply an eye shadow base or simply use your foundation for added texture. The added texture will create stability and give your eye shadow color something to stick to.

Start by choosing three different shades. Apply the medium shade on your lid, from lash line to brow bone, apply darkest color to the crease of your eyelid, and apply the lightest shade just underneath your brow bone for a highlight. This creates a rainbow of colors that are well blended and beautifully arranged. If you are using different shades of colors, be creative, but always use the darkest in the crease of your lid to create an illusion of depth and dimension; and always blend well. After you have applied your rainbow of colors, finish off with eyeliner.

Learning the techniques and secrets of applying make-up can really make a difference to the over-all appearance of your make-up. For some, learning how to apply make-up will be easy; for others, it will take practice. With the invention of new cosmetic products every day, cosmetic manufacturers are making it easier to look our best and spend less time doing it.

Experiment and find what products work best for you. You may like a cream eye shadow, and your friend may like a powder, but no matter what the difference, you need to discover what is best for you. When shopping for cosmetics use these determining factors: skin tone, budget, and time to apply make-up.

Eyebrows

Don't forget your eyebrows! Your eyebrows are a part of your face and should be kept well groomed. The shape and color of your eyebrow can play an important role in enhancing your facial beauty. An eyebrow pencil can be used to fill in eyebrows that look sparse or spotty or are just simply too thin or light in color. Using eyebrow filler can be tricky. Do research before you attempt to groom your eyebrows. There are many eyebrow tools available on the market today. One of the most inventive and creative tools is an eyebrow stencil. An eyebrow stencil can be used to help assure that you are achieving the eyebrow shape you desire.

There are many shapes of brow styles. For example, there is the curved, the angled, the soft angle, the round or the flat style. The best way to choose a style for your face is to study the natural shape of your brow and work from it. Along with eyebrow stencils, you will find other helpful tools like brow powders, brow lighteners, brow pencils, tweezers, razors, brow gels and mousses, brushes, combs, and brow scissors. All these tools are helpful in achieving and maintaining your eyebrow style. Unbelievably, you can even buy eyebrow wigs! In the 1700's they shaved off their eyebrows and glued on eyebrow wigs made from mouse hair!

I recommend using the natural eyebrow you have already been given, and you don't have to spend a lot of time and money creating great looking eyebrows. There are many things within your reach to help you achieve your best look. By using a soft toothbrush, you can keep your brows beautifully shaped and groomed. By using tweezers and scissors you may already have on hand, you can trim and maintain your brows with ease.

Instead of using brow mousse or gel to keep brows in place, simply use hair gel or hair spray by applying it to your toothbrush and combing it onto brow. Or, use a pencil to help guide you to beautiful looking eyebrows instead of high dollar brow stencils. However, don't take for granted that shaping eyebrows is an easy thing to do. It is something that will take time, patience, and practice. A rule of thumb: don't start tweezing without first understanding the technique. Keep these rules in mind when shaping your eyebrows.

The biggest mistake people make in tweezing their eyebrows is tweezing too much. Avoid over plucking. Instead, remove a little at a time. Your mistakes will not grow back over night. To determine the width between your brows, you should know that the space should be equal to or a little wider than the inner corner of your eyes. Once you have determined the width, start removing any stray hairs across the bridge of your nose. When shaping your eyebrows, you can use a pencil for a guideline. Place the pencil at the side of your nose making sure it is held straight up and down. This will also help determine where you should stop plucking between the brows.

Tweeze any brow hairs to the right, left of the pencil, or to make it simple, remove any brow hairs between your eyes. Now, slant the pencil diagonally by holding it next to the corner of your nose and extend it to the outer edge of your eye. This will create a guideline as to where your eyebrow should end. To determine the arch of the brow, look straight into the mirror and follow the middle of your pupil upward into your brow again using your pencil for a guide. Remove a little at a time. Stand back from the mirror and look at what you have done. Make sure each side matches the best you can.

Never tweeze brows from the top but always from underneath. Always pluck your brows in the direction they grow. Don't grab too many hairs at one time. Hold your skin taut as you pluck one hair at a time. This will help ease the pain. If the pain is too much, try using a teething gel to numb the skin around the brow before plucking.

Arch your brows by thinning the brow hairs in moderation until you have achieved the desired arch. Using a magnifying mirror in the natural light will help assure that you are getting all brow hairs. The best place to place your mirror is on a window ledge. Use a good pair of tweezers. Stainless-steel tweezers offer the most precision. Slanted tips are the most popular and work the best. They rest more comfortably against the skin, and provide the advantage needed to nip the hair at its root. After you have achieved your brow style and shape, fill them in with a brow pencil that matches your brow color and groom into place.

Princess Bible Verse

I Peter 3:3-4
"Your beauty should not come from outward adornment, such as braided hair and the wearing of gold jewelry and fine clothes. Instead, it should be that of your inner self, the unfading beauty of a gentle and quiet spirit, which is of great worth in God's sight."

👑 Princess Beauty Tips

There are many tools a princess can use to enhance her beauty. Make-up brushes are a great way to apply make-up to your face and help you look beautiful. There are also many tools you can use to enhance your inward beauty and help you look and feel beautiful: praying, reading the Bible, loving one another, laughing, and enjoying your life.

👑 Princess Confessions

I love the way I look because God made me in his image. God makes me beautiful!

👑 Princess Prayer

Father, I praise you and thank you for your greatness. I thank you that you have given me a free will of choice. I understand that I should acknowledge you in all my ways, even when it comes to my make-up bag. Lord, I do not want to mislead people or cause them to stumble. Help me to be a good representation of you. Thank you for loving me with or without make-up. In Jesus' name, Amen.

👑 Princess Challenge

Wear less make-up and stop relying on it to make you feel beautiful. Go through your make-up bag and determine how you can simplify.

👑 Princess Crown Thought

Wearing make-up enhances your natural beauty, don't wear it like a mask and hide behind it.

Princess Journaling Assignment

What are your feelings about wearing make-up? Do you feel it necessary to make you beautiful?

_____
_____
_____
_____
_____
_____
_____
_____
_____
_____
_____
_____

Write Your Own Prayer:_____
_____
_____
_____
_____
_____

Chapter 8

God and Your Hair

God loves you so much that he has taken the time to decide the color of your hair, the color of your eyes, how your smile should look, the uniqueness of your voice and laugh, and even the placement of dimples on your cheeks. He has skillfully designed every feature about you. Think about this, God loves you so much that he even has the very hairs on your head numbered![1] Yes, your hairs are numbered! Can you believe it? That is amazing! God's word says a woman's hair is her crown of glory and it is her covering.[2] This means you should take pride in the way you take care of your hair. It is like a crown. Your hair belongs to you and is a part of your body. God does not care if you cut it, style it, color it, or even perm it.

However, always keep in mind you are a representative of him so make him proud no matter what you do.

Your hair is made of protein. Protein is the most basic of all the body's building blocks. Protein is what you get from eating eggs, meat, and fish. You should eat enough protein to keep your body and your hair healthy. Hair is built-up in three layers. Most hair grows at a rate of about one-half inch per month, making the ends about two years old at shoulder length. You have 90,000 to 140,000 individual hairs on your head. Redheads have the least at about 90,000. Brown-haired people have about 110,000, and blonde-haired people have the most hair with 140,000 or more.

Hair grows faster during warm weather and at night. Your hair can grow six to seven inches each year. Its growth slows, as you get older. Cutting your hair does not make it grow faster. It only eliminates split ends and gives an illusion of thicker, healthier hair. It is normal to lose a small amount of hair each day. You have young hairs and old hairs on your head. The old is replaced by the new. The normal hair loss varies from fifty to one hundred strands of hair per day.

Having beautiful hair doesn't just happen. It comes by taking good care of it and establishing a beauty regimen that best fits your hair type. It is not always necessary to wash your hair every day, in fact, it is best to wash your hair every two to three days. Although your hair does attract dirt and odors throughout the day, it is a good idea to rinse it with clean water. It is not necessary to use shampoos and conditioners every time you bathe.

There are many different hair types, and by determining your hair type, you can decide how it needs to be cared for each day. There are many types of hair products from which to choose. Most of the time, one is just as good as the other. They all contain about the same ingredients, and do about the same thing. The only difference between hair salon products and other products you buy over the counter is the concentration. Most inexpensive products contain more water and the more expensive less water. It is best to find what products work for you. It is also a good practice to change your products and try a new brand every one to two months. This will eliminate build-up of product on your hair, give your hair a change, and may help with any irritations you may be experience.

Shampoo

Shampoo is used to wash out the dirt and grime. Most shampoos are made with the same ingredients, but it is the amount of water added to the product that makes the difference. It is up to you to find what best fits your hair type and your budget. To use a shampoo, squeeze a quarter-size amount of shampoo onto the palm of your hand and gently rub your hands together. Start at the ends and work your way up. Rinse well and repeat if necessary.

Conditioners

Conditioners are used to restore oil back into your hair. Too much conditioner can work against your hair by causing it to look lifeless, greasy, and become unmanageable. Conditioners help keep your hair healthy, smooth, and can reduce tangles. There are many factors to why your hair needs to be conditioned. Some of those factors include hair that has been damaged by over-processing. Over-processing can include perms, colors, blow drying, hot irons, prolonged sun exposure and chlorine. All of these factors can rob your hair from its natural moisture. To use a conditioner, simply apply a quarter-sized amount of conditioner into the palm of your hand, and work it into the ends of your hair. Rule—only apply from the ears down. Massage the strands of your hair, and pay attention to the ends. Don't apply conditioner directly onto the scalp. The top of your hair doesn't need much conditioner as the strands do. The strands of your hair take the blunt of styling. However, if you have long bangs, applying conditioner to the ends will help keep them smooth and healthy. Conditioners can be applied to help with the detangling of your hair as well as helping repair it. If you have short hair or unmanageable hair, try using a lightweight leave-in conditioning spray.

Deep Conditioning

To keep hair beautiful and shiny, use a deep conditioner once a week. For extra healthy hair, try the hair mask recipe listed in the beauty recipe section at the back of this book once a month. This will help keep your hair looking healthy and give it a boost. You can use your daily conditioner as a deep conditioner by applying as you would when washing, except don't wash it out. Wrap conditioned hair in a towel, and leave in for about twenty minutes. A hot oil treatment is good to strip away all the buildup that is left behind from styling products and even residue from using your shampoos and conditioners. When using a deep conditioner or hot oil treatment always rinse thoroughly.

Shampoo and Conditioner All-in-One

With all the hair care products available, it is easy to become confused. Combining products together makes it more convenient for the consumer and costs less. However, using an all-in-one shampoo may not be the best thing for your hair. If your hair is very damaged and dry, this product will work great. However, if your hair is normal or oily, applying conditioner every time you shampoo is not necessary. Conditioner can create a build-up on your hair and leave it dull and unmanageable. It is a good idea to keep a bottle of all-in-one shampoo and conditioner on hand when your hair does need conditioned.

Styling Products

With the growing number of hair styling products on the market today, it is hard to keep up with them all. There are many new and improved products that will help you achieve your desired hairstyle. The smartest way to know what products will work best for you and your hair type is by asking your hairdresser. Here are some hair products that are easy to use and work well:

- Hair Wax, Gel, Mousse, or Liquid Spray Gel

Used for any length of hair to achieve the stiff, well-defined look.

- Frizz Serum

Used to smooth out the frizz from over-processed hair.

- Temporary Color/Permanent Color/Wash-in-Color

Used to add subtle or dramatic color all over or in designated spots (use color with caution); it is best to let a professional color your hair.

- Hairspray and Spritz Spray

Used to hold hair in place and comes in many different strengths.

Hair Styling Tools

A blow dryer is a great tool to own because of its convenience, but can be harmful to your hair just as any tool that applies heat straight to the hair. When blow drying, keep the blow dryer at least a foot away from your head. Try to avoid placing the dryer directly onto your hair.

A curling iron can be found in many different sizes and shapes, there are irons that make a smooth curl and irons that can make a spiral curl. Instead of placing hair directly into the curling iron mouth, try taking segments of hair and wrapping them around the barrel of the curling iron. Wrap one segment up the barrel and another down the barrel to create layers of curls.

Hot Rollers are used to heat set your hair by selecting strands of hair and wrapping them around a roller. Note: using hot rollers and even curling irons every day can cause your hair to become dry, brittle, and may cause breakage. A great alternative to heat setting your hair is to use sponge or velcro rollers. These work great but take a little extra time to use. Sleeping in rollers or even pulling your hair up into a bun on the top of your head and securing it with a clip can leave beautiful curls for the next day without having to use a heated tool.

A crimper or flat iron is used to achieve a wavy or straight look. This tool can damage your hair and even burn it off. Read all the directions in the package to determine proper use. Before crimping or flat ironing your hair, coat it with a layer of protecting sealer like spray gel, flat ironing smoothing gel, or hair gloss. An iron with a ceramic plate about 1" in width, and temperature control dials will work the best. Start your iron on a lower setting. Never start ironing your hair on the highest setting, and never leave the iron in one place on your hair for very long. Practice using your flat iron or crimper while it is cold before trying it hot.

Combing and Brushing

Your hair needs to be brushed, combed, or picked out daily to remove tangles. Always brush your hair before bedtime to avoid a mess in the morning. If you have long hair, try pinning or tying it up while you sleep. This will avoid any hang-ups the next morning. Brushing your hair over your head will help stimulate hair growth and cause the natural oils to surface for that shiny, healthy look. Too much brushing can also cause hair to look oily and create unwanted split ends.

Learn what works best for your hair type and style. Never use a small-toothed comb or brush on your hair when it is wet. Your hair is very fragile and can break easily. The pulling and tugging can damage your hair making it look frizzy. Use a wide toothed comb or pick instead. Always comb or pick through hair before drying to make styling easier. Rule—remember when you are combing, brushing, or picking your hair, start at the ends and work your way up. Doing this will allow the tangles to fall out easier and will minimize breakage. As a reminder, if God cares enough to number ever hair on your head, shouldn't you care enough to do what is best for your hair? God loves you and your hair.

There are many different styles of brushes and combs in which to choose. A large paddle brush works best for long hair and is great for using while blow drying to achieve that sleek, smooth look. A soft-bristled brush is also great to us as a smoothing tool. However, a soft-bristled brush has a tendency to trap static electricity and cause fly-a-ways. A heated styling brush is a brush lined with metal plating on the inside. It is designed to by used with heat usually a hair dryer. The metal plate heats up and aids in styling. Picks and wide toothed combs are perfect for permed or wet hair. It allows you to comb easily through the hair without pulling out curls or strands.

A small-toothed comb can be used for smoothing and defining, but is most often found in the pocket of a man. There is a special comb used to rat hair. The teeth of the comb are set close together with smaller teeth in between. It works perfectly for defining and adding volume. No matter what style or type of styling tool you may choose, always remember to keep them clean. Soak your hair utensils in a sink full of hot soapy water at least once a week to remove all the grit and grime from styling and them free from hair.

Hair Accessories

There are numerous hair accessories on the market. Hair accessories include hair combs, hair barrettes, hair clips, bobby pins, headbands, scarves, bandanas, hair ribbons, banana clips, french roll combs, ponytail holders, hair bows, and so many more. When you are shopping for hair accessories, it can become over-whelming. Finding the right package of ponytail holders can be a challenge. However, there are a few tips to keep in mind when shopping for accessories. Consider your hair type, the style you want to achieve, the cost, color, and how often you will be using the accessory. You might even want to take a picture along to the store to help you decide. Looking through hairstyling magazines will give you ideas of new and creative ways to use hair accessories. Keeping three different sizes of ponytail holders on hand is a good idea. You can use large bands for larger ponytails with more hair, small bands for smaller ponytails, and small rubber bands for those very small ponytails or braids. Rule—never pull hair bands, no matter what size, from your hair. By doing so you could risk damaging and even tangling your hair. The best way to remove a small rubber band is to cut it out. Just like your hair brushes and combs, your hair accessories should be kept clean. Throw away broken or worn-out hair accessories. A princess always looks her best from crown to toe.

Common Hair Problems

Everyone has a hair problem of some kind. Common hair problems can include over-processed hair, oily hair, dry hair, dry flaky scalp or dandruff, or small blisters on the scalp. Just like your skin, your hair also has a type. It may be dry, oily, coarse, wiry, or curly. You may have split ends, naturally wavy hair, or baby fine hair. A number of different factors like coloring, straightening, using a hair dryer, hot rollers, curling irons, or any kind of heated styling tool can cause dry hair. In addition, chlorine pools and too much exposure to the sun can take a toll on your hair. Dry, damaged hair is sometimes hard to restore and most often needs a good haircut to help get it back into shape. Dry hair can be treated with deep conditioners, and a lot of daily maintenance. Use wisdom and make healthy choices for your hair.

Oily hair is usually stringy hair. If you have oily hair, it is a good practice to wash your hair daily. Don't use a heavy shampoo and only use a conditioner as needed, maybe once a week. Oily hair needs to rinsed thoroughly and kept as clean as possible. Sometimes oily hair can result from using the wrong kind of products or by not washing properly. Brush your hair before washing. This will stir up oil and soil particles that can be easily removed when washing. If you need a detangling agent, try using a leave-in conditioning spray. If you are prone to having oily hair, find out what works best to keep it under control and looking its best.

Coarse, wiry hair is sometimes associated with naturally curly or wavy hair. Having your hair trimmed regularly and keeping it clean will help keep your hair looking beautiful. Over washing will cause your hair to look dry. Try washing your hair every other day and be sure to use a conditioner every time you shampoo. Don't try to straighten it or hide it in a ponytail. Instead, learn how to care for it.

Naturally, wavy hair is a girl's dream but it could also be a girl's nightmare.

Split ends can occur from styling, brushing, or combing. Unfortunately, they cannot be helped; but by proper brushing, cutting and conditioning, you can minimize them and keep them under control. Try to have your hair trimmed at least every six weeks; this will help keep hair healthy and split ends to a minimum.

Baby fine hair is hard to manage and usually has the fly-a-ways. This hair type needs more protein to give it that body it needs. Using a protein rinse will help. Avoid over brushing and conditioning. Too much brushing can stimulate more oil and cause it to be more unmanageable. Baby fine hair doesn't need regular conditioning unless it is dry and damaged. Baby fine hair is also hard to perm. To create that extra body and bounce you need use a root lifter or mousse. Blow drying and brushing your hair flipped over your head will also create body. Use your hands when styling to create lift and volume. Allow your baby fine hair to air-dry for more manageability.

Dandruff is shedded scalp scales. Everyone sheds scales, but some shed more than others. When shedding becomes excessive, it is often called dandruff. Most simple cases of dandruff are easy to control by frequent shampooing. A special dandruff product may also be required. Those white flakes could also be caused by an allergic reaction to a hair care product that you may be using. Products with too much alcohol, like hair sprays and hair gels, can cause scalp irritation.

Anyone can have good hair. Don't become discouraged by your hair type. Ask your hairdresser for ways to care for and manage your hair type or look for experts online. Great looking hair starts by knowing how to care for it and then making it a priority.

Tips for Great Looking Hair

- Gently brush your hair before washing to remove any tangles, dust, or hair spray.
- Wet your hair thoroughly with water before applying your shampoo.
- Only use a quarter-size amount of shampoo
- Don't place shampoo or conditioner directly to the top of your head.
- Rinse hair thoroughly to remove all product. Long hair will need extra rinse time.
- Only apply conditioner from the ears down.
- Have your hair trimmed every six weeks.
- Apply a conditioner at least every other day depending on your hair type.
- After washing and rinsing, wring out excess water and gently towel dry.
- Pat your hair with a towel instead of rubbing it together.
- To absorb moisture, quickly wrap a dry towel around your head and leave on for a few minutes.
- If possible, avoid brushing your hair when it is wet. But if you have to, use a large toothed comb and start at the ends.
- Always keep your hair clean, well groomed, and out of your face.
- Along with your smile, your hair is something people notice the most.
- Healthy hair and scalp means perfect hair conditions.
- Avoid over processing, over-heating, and over-styling.
- Only use a small amount of hair styling products to avoid extra build-up.
- Mix vinegar and water in equal parts as a final rinse once a week for squeaky clean hair.
- Eat a healthy diet with plenty of fruits, vegetable, and protein foods to help keep hair healthy and shiny.
- Exercise to increase circulation and blood flow and encourage hair growth.
- Avoid long exposures in the sun.
- Don't wash your hair before going out into a full day of the sun. The natural oil in the hair helps protect it from the sun and pollution damage.
- Don't dry hair when it is completely wet, instead let your hair air dry at least eighty percent before applying heat.
- Use tangle-free hair bands to avoid any hang-ups.
- Brush through hair often to keep it tangle-free and looking great.

Face Shapes and Hair Styles

Round Face

If you have a round face, it is short and broad, with full cheeks. Try to give your face a lengthened look by adding height to the top of your head and keeping the sides very close to your face.

The Oval Face

If you have this shape, your face will be long and narrow. Try a soft, rounded hairstyle with lots of fullness at the sides. Avoid straight hair, tight curls, and adding height to the crown.

The Square Face

The square face has a forehead and a jaw line equally wide, very angular or boxy. A soft hairstyle will assist in rounding out those straight lines. Try a medium or long cut, which will modify the corners, or the very soft curls, which take away from the same squareness. Avoid wearing bangs cut straight across your forehead. This will also emphasize the squareness of your face.

The Heart-Shaped Face

If your face has a wide forehead, widens slightly at the cheeks, and narrows at the jaw almost to a point at the chin, then you are a heart. Fullness is needed in the front, like a pageboy or a flip hairstyle. Avoid off the face hairstyles.

The Triangular-Shaped Face

If you have a narrow forehead, with wider cheeks, and even wider jaw and chin lines, you have a triangular-shaped face. Since your forehead is usually short and narrow, find a hairstyle to widen the area at the temples, and one that has a full crown to balance your large jaw line. Let your hair be full instead of brushing it all back or pulling it back off your face.[3]

In summary, your hair and your face are beautiful no matter what type, style, or shape you may have. These face shapes are the most common, although there are many more your face shape could be classified by. You could also have a combination of two face shapes together. The fact is God loves you no matter what you look like. He has made everyone in a unique and special way. Be happy with what God has given you, make the best of it by taking good care of yourself, and learn how to enhance your best features by choosing the right colors and right hairstyles. You are special, you are wonderful, and you are beautiful!

Princess Bible Verse

Matthew 10:30

"But even the very hairs of your head are all numbered."

Princess Beauty Tip

A princess always keeps her hair shiny and beautiful. She can use a hairbrush to create a smooth and sleek look. The Bible is much like a hairbrush; it is full of words that can help remove and smooth out the tangles in your life.

Princess Confessions

God cares about me and has numbered every hair on my head. He knows everything about me, big or small. I am special to God and he loves me.

Princess Prayer

Lord, you are awesome and perfect in all your ways! It truly amazes me that you took the time to number every hair on my head. You really care about everything. Thank you for numbering the hairs on my head and giving me hair to enjoy. Help me to always look my best and to learn how to care for my hair in a way that would be pleasing in your sight. In Jesus' name, Amen.

Princess Challenge

Take pride in the appearance of your hair and spend extra time each day caring for it.

Princess Crown Thought

A princess wears a crown on her head and always has well-groomed hair to cushion it.

Princess Journaling Assignment

How much time do you spend caring for your hair? List all the products you are using and ask yourself if they are all necessary. Write down the steps of how you achieve and maintain your hair style. Are you constantly changing your hairstyle? Why?

_____

_____

_____

_____

_____

_____

_____

_____

_____

_____

_____

_____

_____

_____

_____

_____

_____

_____

Write Your Own Prayer:

Chapter 9

God and Your Hands and Feet

God needs every part of your body in order to carry out his work on this earth, and each part of your body has been created in a unique way. Most all of us have hands and feet. Your hands and feet can be used to help God in many ways. One way the Bible mentions is by praying for the sick.[1] Another way is by lifting your hands to God and glorifying his holy name. There are many ways you can use your hands for Jesus. You can play the piano, type a newsletter, clean windows, cook a meal, write a story, or just simply pray. Your hands are important and valuable and should be used and taken care of with much wisdom and care. Your hands are more exposed to hardships in the way of weather, work, and repeated washing than any other part of your body. Your hands need special attention and special care to help keep them looking healthy and smooth.

Keep your hands clean and free from dirt, grime, and germs by washing often. When washing your hands, use warm water and pat dry instead of rubbing. Protect your hands when working by wearing gloves. Make a habit of wearing gloves in cold weather. This will help protect them from the extreme cold. Apply hand lotion before putting on your gloves to moisten while you work or play. Applying a hand lotion after each washing and at the first sign of dryness will help prevent chapping problems. Apply a layer of lotion to your hands before bedtime and cover them with lightweight cotton gloves. When you awake in the morning you will have soft and smooth skin. Lava soap is a great abrasive soap to use on your hands and feet to remove stubborn stains. Make you sure you keep it away from water when it is not in use. Too much moister will cause it to melt away. Like your hair and your skin, your hands need a deep conditioning treatment at least once a week. Paraffin wax is a treatment you can use. Refer to the princess beauty treatment section at the back of this book to learn how to sue a paraffin wax treatment.

Most women like long, beautiful, and manicured fingernails. However, having long fingernails won't make them beautiful. You can use expensive nail polish and the most attractive color you can find, but if your nails are chipped and broken, color and expense won't make a difference. Take a good look at your hands and nails and ask yourself this question, "What can I do to improve the appearance of my hands and nails?" If your nails are not as pretty as you would like them to be, make time each week for a manicure. A manicure can greatly improve the appearance of your nails. Schedule an easy but effective nail care program that will fit into your daily/weekly schedule. It only takes a few minutes each day to keep great looking nails.

How to do a Manicure

Use a nail polish remover on a cotton ball to remove old polish. Soak a cotton ball with remover and hold it against the nail for a few seconds until the cotton ball starts to slip, then wipe the nail clean. File nails by using an emery board and file in only one direction. Never file back and forth, this causes the nail to crack and split. Do not file deep into the corners since this weakens the nail and can be painful if you file too deep. Soak nails in lukewarm, soapy water. Remove after about three to five minutes, dry your fingertips, and gently push the cuticle back with a towel or the pad of your finger. For extra softness, add a drop of olive or almond oil to your soaking water. Use a cotton-tipped orangewood stick gently pushing back the cuticle starting from one side of the nail and working your way around. Push very gently and keep cuticle moist at all times. If you have a hangnail, trim it with a pair of clippers instead of trying to bite or pull it off.

Before applying nail polish, clean nails with a moist cotton ball to remove any oils. Let your nails dry for a few moments. Apply a clear base coat. Start with your thumb, then the little finger, the ring, middle and index fingers. This allows each finger to move out of the way for the next one and keeps from smearing the base coat. Apply two coats of polish, but be careful to let each application dry thoroughly before applying the next one. If not, you may see air bubbles underneath. Seal with a clear top coat. To give your nails an extra layer of protection, polish slightly over the nail tip.

Touch up your manicure as soon as you see the first signs of a chip. Add a new coat of polish or just a top coat to prevent any more chipping and to add to the strength of your nails. Nails grow at a rate of one-fourth of an inch per month, so a new nail will be replaced in about four months, depending on the individual. Your nail grows faster in youth and decreases with age. Anything to stimulate circulation will encourage nail growth, like buffing, massaging, or any activity of the fingers, such as typing or piano playing. Nails grow faster in the summer and during pregnancy. To maintain healthy, long nails you must eat well-balanced meals.

Pedicures

Who doesn't like to have their feet rubbed and pampered? The key to having great looking feet starts with a pedicure. A pedicure is a manicure for your toenails. Of course, a pedicure alone will not cause you to have great looking feet; many factors will play along with it. Applying thick lotions to your heels and to the balls of your feet will help keep them soft and smooth. Keeping your toenails free from dirt and grime and removing any old chipped nail polish will also guarantee beautiful toenails. People are most likely to notice your toenails and your feet in the summertime when flip-flops and sandals are worn. Nevertheless, no matter what the season, always make sure your toenails are neatly groomed and manicured.

A pedicure is similar to a manicure, with a few alterations. A big tub will be needed for soothing and soaking your feet. A bathtub will serve as a great place to start your pedicure. Before soaking your feet, remove the dead skin by brushing with a scrub brush or a footstone. Soaking your feet will soften them up and make it easier to push back those cuticles. It will also make it easier to trim away rough edges around the nail. After soaking, remove feet and towel dry. Now is the perfect time to push back cuticles, trim away rough edges, file and shape your nails. When filing and trimming your toenails, remember that straight across is better than rounding and short is better than long. Finally, after you have pushed your cuticles back, filed and trimmed, lavish your feet with lots of lotion paying close attention to the heels and the balls of your feet. Congratulations! You have successfully completed your pedicure. A special note to those of you with sandpaper feet—make it a habit to lavish your feet with your favorite foot cream every night before bedtime or before you put on your favorite pair of socks.

Common Nail Problems

Dry, brittle nails do not retain moisture as well as normal nails, so it is up to you to replace their moisture. Try soaking your nails in lukewarm water every night for a couple of minutes and then rub them with Vaseline. In addition, you might try a weekly soak in warm olive oil. Nail polish remover is very drying to the nail, so use only when needed. It is better to touch up your polish instead of removing your polish every time.

Soft Nails

If your nails are soft, try a nail hardener with protein. You can purchase an acrylic shield or a protective base coat with a vinyl nail guard in it. Keep these acrylic shields on your nails at all times to build up their strength and try to keep your hands out of water as much as possible. Wear gloves and keep your nails polished.

Hangnails

Hangnails are a result of dry cuticles. If you have a problem with hangnails, try using a cuticle cream regularly to prevent them from forming and gently clip hangnails as soon as they appear. If you don't have cuticle cream, use hand lotion, Vaseline, almond oil, or olive oil.

Nail Biting

Nail biting can result in damaged nails, not to mention it can be very embarrassing. To cure nail biting, first, determine when you bite your nails the most. Are you biting your nails because you are under stress? Do you bite your nails when you feel out of control? Or do you bite your nails when you are nervous or anxious? Most people bite their nails because there are nervous or anxious about something in their life. The Bible tells us to not be anxious.

Do not fret or have any anxiety about anything, but in every circumstance and in everything, by prayer and petition (definite requests), with thanksgiving, continue to make your wants known to God. And God's peace [shall be yours, that tranquil state of a soul assured of its salvation through Christ, and so fearing nothing from God and being content with its earthy lot of whatever sort that is, that peace] which transcends all understanding shall garrison and mount guard over your hearts and minds in Christ Jesus.

Philippians 4:6

If anxiety is your problem, put a stop to it. Quote this scripture and release your faith. This scripture also states that we are to give our prayers, supplications, and thanksgiving to God and his peace shall come over us. If you are struggling with nail biting and want to stop, make your request known unto God and he will help you. Start thanking him now for helping you stop biting your nails.

If you do bite your nails, try keeping them polished and well-manicured. You might even apply an acrylic nail to help you avoid biting. They will look a lot better and you will be inspired to quit when you see how pretty they can look when kept well groomed. Don't give up and don't lose heart; you can stop biting your nails with a little time and patience. Trust God and he will take care of you.

White Spots/Yellow Nails

If you have a problem with white spots, it may be a sign of stress. Stress affects your body, soul, and spirit. Stress puts a strain on your body and creates a force that will lead you into destruction. Try eating more gelatin products like Jell-O and you will eventually see them disappear. Yellow nails are a result of smoking, medication, or nail polish pigment. Always apply a base coat to protect your nails from stains caused from polishing. Yellow nails can also be a sign of a nutritional deficiency. Check with your doctor or health food store consultant for help on determining the cause.

Do's and Don'ts of Nail Care

Do keep all your nails free from dirt and grime.

Do match your fingernail and toenail polish.

Do maintain your pedicure to assure great looking feet and toenails.

Do apply lotion to feet and toenails after bathing.

Do push back cuticles around the toenail.

Do trim and file toenails straight across.

Do take pride in all parts of your body, including your feet.

Do use a small, stiff brush to scrub your nails.

Do keep your nails neatly shaped.

Do keep an emery board handy.

Do roll things to the edge of the table to pick them up.

Do soak dry and brittle nails in warm olive oil up to fifteen minutes.

Do soak discolored nails in lemon juice or hydrogen peroxide for about fifteen minutes.

Do use a pumice stone or heel exfoliate brush to rub and soften feet.

Do correct foot problems at the first sign of trouble.

Don't allow your nails to grow longer than you can maintain.

Don't neglect your feet!

Don't use your nails as tools.

Don't bite loose cuticles or pull them with your teeth or finger nails.

Don't leave chipped or faded polish on your nails. Repair as soon as you can.

Don't bite your nails, toenails, or fingernails.

Princess Manicure

Before you start your manicure, take a look at your nails and answer these questions. Circle your answer.

My hands are smooth and soft.	*Always*	*Sometimes*	*Never*
My nails are filed and well-shaped.	*Always*	*Sometimes*	*Never*
My nails are chipped, broken, and uneven in length.	*Always*	*Sometimes*	*Never*
I bite my nails.	*Always*	*Sometimes*	*Never*
I am quick to repair my nail polish when the color starts to chip or fade.	*Always*	*Sometimes*	*Never*
I use my nails as tools.	*Always*	*Sometimes*	*Never*
My cuticles are dry and cracking.	*Always*	*Sometimes*	*Never*
My finger and toenails are kept clean and free from dirt.	*Always*	*Sometimes*	*Never*
My feet are kept soft and smooth.	*Always*	*Sometimes*	*Never*

How can I improve the overall appearance of my nails, hands, and feet? Explain.

_____

_____

_____

Princess Word Scramble

All these words are related to the things you use to take care of your body from crown to toe. Can you unscramble the letters to find out what they are? Draw a line to connect your answers.

A R B R H S H I U	SHAMPOO
B T O H O U T S H	CONDITIONOR
B M C O	LOTION
A P O S	LIPSTICK
O M P H A S O	NAIL POLISH
D T C O N E R I O N I	MASCARA
W L T O E	BLUSH
S W A H T O H O L C	HAIRBRUSH
N L I A P L I O S H	SOAP
N L I A L I P E R P C S	COMB
S C R A A M A	NAIL CLIPPERS
L H U S B	TOOTHBRUSH
P S T K C I I L	TOWEL
Y E E S W H O D A	WASH CLOTH
O O T H T P S T A E	EYE SHADOW

God and Your Hands and Feet

👑 Princess Beauty Tips

A princess always makes sure her fingernails and toenails are well-manicured. She can use a fingernail file to maintain beautiful looking nails. The Bible gives us wisdom on how we can file and trim away unrighteousness so we can maintain a beautiful well-manicured life that is pleasing in the sight of the Lord.

👑 Princess Confessions

I am the handiwork of the Lord handcrafted and created in His image. I will serve the Lord and use my hands, feet, and life for Him forever. I will be the best representative for Christ Jesus I can be.

👑 Princess Prayer

Lord, how beautiful you are! I praise you and thank you for giving me hands and feet to praise you in all I do. Help me to use my hands and feet to glorify you. I confess today that everything my hands shall touch will prosper, and every step I take will be in you. My hands will praise you and I will lift them continually in praise and thanksgiving of your goodness toward me. In Jesus' name, Amen.

👑 Princess Challenge

Keep your hands, feet, and nails clean and well-groomed. Take the time to do a manicure and pedicure once a week.

👑 Princess Crown Thought

Looking good depends a lot on how you care for yourself and choose to present it to others. The spirit of excellence never goes out of style. Straighten you crown princess, you are destined to reign.

👑 Princess Journaling Assignment

Your body is the temple of the Holy Spirit. In other words, it's where Jesus lives. Are you keeping His house clean? How can you take better care of your hands and feet, and your temple so that you may be ready for every good work? You matter. Take care of you. It is your responsibility. Write your thoughts.

_____

_____

_____

_____

_____

_____

_____

_____

_____

_____

_____

_____

_____

_____

_____

_____

_____

Write Your Own Prayer:

Chapter 10

God and Your Smile

Did you know there is no other smile like yours on earth? How would you like to create millions and millions of smiles that are in no way alike? God has done just that. Just like our bodies, personalities, looks, and laughs are uniquely designed, so are our smiles. Have you ever heard the expression, "Smile, it makes your face happy"? Did you know it takes seventy muscles to frown and only ten to smile; not to mention frowning causes wrinkles. Your smile is usually the first thing people notice about you. We use our mouth to speak words, but we also use our mouth to express our feelings. I like the scripture, *"from the abundance of the heart the mouth speaketh," (Matthew 12:34)*. I like to think of this scripture not only as words, but also as expressions. If your heart is happy inside, your mouth is going to show it by smiling. If you are unhappy inside, your mouth is going to show it by frowning or in some other less attractive way. When is the last time you tried on your smile? Have you worn it lately? One thing about a smile, it never goes out of style and it always matches everything you wear. You have a beautiful smile; wear it!

Your smile is not only maintained from the heart, but it is also maintained by the way you take care of your teeth. Your teeth are expecting your full attention to care for them. Teeth will not take care of themselves, so you will have to invest time in caring for them. Keeping your teeth brushed at least twice a day will not make them any straighter or even any whiter, but it will keep them healthy. A healthy smile will determine how much time you spend on caring for your teeth. Try brushing your teeth after every meal if possible. Doing this will remove the leftover food particles from your teeth and keep your breath smelling fresh. If you are unable to brush your teeth after every meal, make it a practice to brush in the morning when you awake and in the evening before bedtime.

Just like leaving make-up on your face overnight can cause skin problems, so cannot brushing your teeth cause teeth and gum problems. The main cause of tooth decay is poor dental hygiene. Brushing, flossing, regular visits to the dentist and proper, healthy nutrition play a large roll in how your smile will sparkle.

Eating and drinking healthy foods can keep your teeth healthy. Just like your body benefits from a healthy diet, so do your teeth. Avoid drinking sugared drinks and replace those drinks with lots of water. In addition, eating foods that are high in sugar like chocolates, candies, and other sweets can cause a build-up on your teeth and could later cause cavities. Choose eating healthy foods like apples, oranges, bananas, and a variety of vegetables. Eat those foods that will benefit your total body image.

Maintaining a Healthy Smile

In early history, dental care wasn't at your fingertips. There were very few, if any dentists in practice, and if there were, people were afraid of them. People did not have the tools or the knowledge that we have today when it comes to caring for the teeth. When they were in serious pain, they often just removed the problem. Women who had missing teeth, would stuff their cheeks with corks so that their faces would look plump and fuller. They used course linen clothes as toothbrushes and pumice stones to remove unwanted stains. Dentist in those days recommended a mixture of sugar and honey to clean teeth – no wonder they had so many teeth missing! One of the most common teeth cleaning practices was the use of mixtures of crushed bone mixed with fruit peel, or burned alum mixed with ground rosemary. Knowing all this, you should hug your toothbrush daily and thank God for giving wisdom in our time to improve dental care.

Brush your teeth with a whitening agent once in the morning to remove bad breath and once in the evening before bedtime. You can also sprinkle your toothpaste with baking soda to help with whitening. Apply a pea-sized amount onto the end of your toothbrush. Toothpaste is to be used sparingly and is mostly for freshening breath. Start brushing by placing the brush alongside the teeth, with the bristles pointing toward the gums. Brush gently and in small, circular motions. Avoid applying a lot of pressure. Too much pressure could cause gum recession and gum bleeding. Don't be afraid to brush all your teeth. Reach with your toothbrush all the way to the back of your mouth in order to brush those hard to reach places. Floss at least once a day. This will help remove food particles.

Removing food from between teeth will also help prevent bad breath. Another way to prevent bad breath is to brush the top of your tongue each time your brush your teeth. For a quick breath freshener try breath mints, eating an apple, or chewing sugar free gum. Remember to visit your dentist every six months for a thorough cleaning and dental check-up.

Your mouth is full of more than just teeth and is used for more than just eating and drinking. Inside your mouth you will also find a tongue. Your tongue is an organ that plays an important role in the health of your body and the outcome of your life. Inside your mouth flows out words; words are very powerful, magnetic containers that contain the force of life or death. The words you speak can bring life or they can bring death. Proverbs 18:21 lets us know the tongue has the power of life and death. Your tongue can be used as a weapon against yourself or against others, and the words that come out of it do matter. God knows everything about your life from the beginning to the end. Don't let your words hinder your progress. Guard every word that comes out of your mouth. Say only positive things about your future, your health, your well-being, and the well-being of others.

It is your choice to speak good things or bad things. Choose to speak words that are filled with life and love. But no matter how hard you try to guard your words James 3:8 tells us that the tongue can never be tamed. *"But the human tongue can be tamed by no man. It is a restless (undisciplined, irreconcilable) evil, full of deadly poison."* Make a choice to speak good things about yourself. The next time you look at your reflection in the mirror, say to it: "I am beautiful! I am special! I am smart! I am loved! I am the healed of the Lord and it shall come to pass that I will prosper in life!" By speaking good words about yourself, you will find it brings strength and encouragement to your soul. Proverbs 12:18 says,

"There are those who speak rashly, like the piercing of a sword, but the tongue of the wise brings healing." When you choose to make negative confessions about yourself, you are piercing yourself with a sword. If you could see your spirit, you would probably see holes gushing with life. By speaking negatively about yourself and saying things like, "I'm not pretty," "I'm not good enough," Or, "I'm not smart enough," you are piercing your spirit. The same goes for speaking bad things about other people; you are piercing them with your words. Rule of thumb—think before you speak. Before you can change the way you speak, you must change the way you think.

"For out of the fullness (the overflow, the superabundance) of the heart the mouth speaks. The good man from his inner good treasure flings forth good things, and the evil man out of his inner evil storehouse flings forth evil things. But I tell you, on the day of judgment men will have to give account for every idle (inoperative, nonworking) word they speak. For by your words you will be justified and acquitted, and by your words you will be condemned and sentenced".

Matthew 12:34-36

This passage of scripture is very powerful. You are held accountable for every idle word that goes out of your mouth. Your words set you up for good or for evil. You have to make a choice to renew your mind and fill your heart with the Word of God. This is the only way you will be able to start thinking and speaking good things about yourself and others. Without the Word of God in your heart, there is no good thing; everything that is good comes from above.[1] God has no evil in his heart; therefore, if your heart is filled with Jesus, you will also be filled with good things and good words.

By reading the word of God and knowing what it says about you, you will always be full of wisdom to speak and think of good things. The book of Proverbs is full of wisdom on how you should control your tongue. It also tells teaches you valuable lessons on speaking good words. Words are very powerful and they come from the depths of your heart. God has given you the power of words. Not only will God's word make a difference in your life, but your choice of words will also make a difference in the outcome of your life. Choose to put good things into your thinking so that only good things will come out of your mouth. Stop listening to music or watching TV programs that are filling your spirit with the wrong words. Think about the importance of those words in which you are listening.

Benefits of Speaking Good Words

Positive words can bring life. Matthew 12:34

Your words will promote health. Proverbs 12:18

Your words will cause you to eat well. Proverbs 13:2

Your words will preserve your life. Proverbs 13:3

Your words will turn away wrath. Proverbs 15:1

A wholesome tongue is a tree of life. Proverbs 15:4

Your words will bring joy. Proverbs 15:23

Your words will make your bones healthy. Proverbs 15:30

Your words bring sweetness to the soul and health to the bones. Proverbs 16:24

Good words will satisfy your stomach. Proverbs 18:20

Good words will bring you blessing. Deuteronomy 11:26

Speaking God's word will bring you nothing but blessing and honor. You are victorious by the words of your mouth. You are destined for greatness, but the words of your mouth will determine that destiny. Study the book of Proverbs for more wisdom on the goodness of speaking God's words. Choose today to speak words of life no matter how you may feel. You have to make yourself think and say good things. Turn off the channel of negative thinking, tune into the channel of God's word, and your speaking will turn onto words of life. Guard your mouth, your tongue, and your heart with all diligence; from out of it springs the issues of life.[2]

Princess Bible Verse

Proverbs 15:30
"A cheerful look brings joy to the heart, and good news gives health to the bones."

♛ Princess Beauty Tips

A princess is never completely dressed without a smile. She always has a smile on her face and a kind word to say. A smile is a great way to accent the color of happiness in your life. From the abundance of your heart, your mouth should radiate with a smile and kindness.

♛ Princess Confessions

I will make the choice to speak uplifting and encouraging words about myself and about others. The joy of the Lord is my strength, and by his strength I am strong enough to control my tongue and my thoughts.

♛ Princess Prayer

Lord, thank you for your smile and happiness over me. I pray for your help to resist the temptation of being rude and critical to myself and to others. Help me to smile and speak good things. Father, sometimes it is hard to smile and I ask you to help me during those times when I don't feel like smiling at all. Thank You for the love you give to me every day. In Jesus' name, Amen.

♛ Princess Challenge

Smile more! Take the time to smile at someone you don't know and say something nice.

♛ Princess Crown Thought

Did you know that only 30 percent of people smile all the time? The other 70 percent are frowning. What percentile do you fit in? What things make you smile?

Princess Journaling Assignment

How often do you smile? What makes you happy? How do you think you can improve the way you speak to others and to yourself? Are you kind to others and following the golden rule of treating others the way you would like to be treated? Write about what is in your heart that makes you do what you do? Frown or Smile.

Write Your Own Prayer:

Chapter 11

God and Your Closet

If anyone were to look in your closet, they would probably find it stuffed with clothes and more clothes. Most women have more clothes than they will ever need or wear. They spend endless hours shopping for the right blouse or the right dress for that special occasion. There is nothing wrong with looking nice and dressing in fine clothes. The problem comes when a person puts all their energy into dressing up the outside and no energy into dressing up the inside. We are bombarded with fashion. Everywhere we turn, we see a world of clothes, shoes, and accessories at our fingertips. Americans are fascinated with looking their best and catching the newest fads and fashions as soon as they go on the market. There are many runway shows were beautiful fashion models model the latest fashion designs. Women spend billions of dollars each year on things to beautify themselves on the outside, and spend pennies on improving the way they look on the inside. They go shopping for more, and once they bring it home, they have nowhere to put it, or three more just like it.

There is nothing wrong with being attracted to beautiful things. But don't allow beautiful things to make you happy. Some could have a closet full of beautiful clothes and never feel happy. You can walk in a pair of $500 shoes, but without God in your life, you won't get very far. God does care how you dress. You are a representation of his son Jesus Christ. If you are a born-again believer, then you are an ambassador of Christ. Therefore, what you wear should reflect what is inside. If you have Jesus in your life and want to be a good representative of him, start examining your wardrobe. It does matter how you represent yourself because others are watching you.

There are many ways you can dress stylish and modestly. No one likes to catch a glimpse of someone's bottom crack peaking over the top of a pair of low-rise jeans. No one wants to see someone's belly hanging out. No one wants to witness someone's cleavage being revealed by a low-cut blouse. No one wants to know what style or color of undergarments you wear by having it revealed by something too short or too low. Dressing to expose yourself is not attractive. There are areas of your body that are meant to be kept concealed and covered.

Don't pattern your fashion style after the pop star on the cover of a magazine. Be yourself by creating your own style. Wearing clothes is a way to express who you are. You may be a jean and t-shirt kind of girl or you may be someone who likes to dress up all the time. No matter what your style, make sure it is created with the ideas of God in mind. You should dress professionally and modestly for God, not as a requirement, but out of respect for him and others. There is a time and a place to lounge around, but try to do it in the privacy of your home where no one can see you.

Allow God into your closet and allow the Holy Spirit to convict you of each piece of clothing you own. Get rid of all those items that are too tight and too revealing. You can be stylish and modest at the same time. God cares about how you look and how you present yourself. You never know who is watching from a distance, and you want your life to be a living testimony to others and not cause them to stumble. You can cause others to stumble by the way you choose to act, speak, and the way you dress. You should stand out in a crowd, not blend in. You live in this world but you are not of it. Put off the world's way of thinking and dressing, and strive to be pleasing to God in every area of your life, including your closet.

You are a fashion statement – fashioned after, created, and designed by the fashion designer –God. God is your fashion designer. You were created in his image and fashioned after his likeness[1]. Everyone longs to be beautiful, look nice, wear designer clothes, and fine jewelry, and indeed, these things may help enhance one's beauty, but it does not determine beauty. God has fashioned and designed you differently than anyone else. He has created people in all shapes, sizes, and colors. However, it is how you decide to wear your design that determines your fashion statement. You can wear beautiful clothes, and there is nothing wrong with that, but when you allow your outward appearance to determine who you are, then you have lost all sense of true beauty. Beauty is not defined by how much your new black dress cost or how great you look in it. Beauty is defined by how you package that expensive black dress by the way you choose to wear it. Let your beauty shine from within – true beauty comes from the heart of a person. You have been created to be beautiful. Make your own fashion statement and stand out by simply being who God created you to be.

Your style is about how you present yourself to others. It is an expression of how you see yourself. Style gives you the power to put a definition behind your name. It describes who you are. Style is a lot more than about the clothes you choose to wear, or the way you choose to wear your hair and make-up. It is all about whom you are—your character, your attitude, your confidence, your self-esteem, your integrity, your faith. Style is all about knowing who you are and a lot about personality. Only God can help you create a style that will never blend in with the fads and fashions of today, changing from one day to the next. And he will help you develop a style that will cause others to look at you and desire what you have. Jesus is the only stylist who can design a garment, an attitude, or a strong character that fits you. Turn someone's head and attention by wearing the garments of salvation and the robe of righteousness. Don't let your closet or the way you choose to dress reflect the world. A believer should dress appropriately in a way that makes them stand out in a crowd. There are many famous fashion designers in the world. Who are you letting influence the way you dress? Let God be your fashion designer, and be influenced by his word and by his ways of how to dress for success.

♛ Wardrobe Planning

Color plays an important role in choosing your cosmetics and in choosing your wardrobe. Never buy clothes or accessories unless the color of your purchase is keyed to your wardrobe plan. A good wardrobe revolves around a few essential clothes that fit your body, personality, lifestyle, and budget. The ideal wardrobe is a small group of clothing coordinated in color, fabric, and shape, with all items being interchangeable. It can consist of as few as five pieces or as many as twenty. What woman doesn't like to go shopping for new clothes? But when you are not sure of what colors, styles, and lines work best on you, shopping can be difficult.

Dressing well is not a matter of having many clothes, wearing expensive clothes, or even wearing the latest fashions. The secret of being well dressed is in choosing clothes that are right for you and your activities. If you don't have a plan for adding new clothes to your wardrobe, you may wind up with a closet full of clothes, but nothing to wear. With a well-planned wardrobe, you will not have to spend a lot of time wondering what to wear. Clothes, made up of mostly separates, can be matched into many combinations. Plan your wardrobe around neutral colors. Neutral colors are whites, grays, black, navy, beiges, and browns. Choose neutrals to harmonize with your seasonal palette and keep neutrals in mind when adding other colors to your wardrobe. When planning your wardrobe, it may sound like a good idea to throw out your clothes and start over. There is no doubt that there are probably clothes in your closet that need to be thrown out. It will take time and patience to inventory the clothing in your closet. But in the end it will be well worth it. Look into your closet and examine each piece of clothing you own. Acknowledge the Lord as you go and ask for his guidance.[2]

Start by taking everything out of bags, boxes or drawers, and off hangers. Try everything on, looking at it carefully, style, fit, attractiveness, and condition. Try on your favorite outfits first, and analyze why they are your favorites. Judge it by the fit, color, and style. Use your favorites as items to build your coordinated wardrobe. Mix and match other pieces with your favorites and try new combinations. Experiment with various accessories while you are evaluating each item. Sort your wardrobe into three groups: in style, in season, and in good condition. Your closet should only house your working wardrobe. Clothes that fit, do not need repair, and that have been worn many times during the past year are wearables. Store, recycle, or give away items that you no longer wear. As a rule of thumb, if you haven't worn it in a year, get rid of it. Most likely, the item is already out of date or no longer fits.

Secondly, after going through all your clothes and accessories, including your shoes, start organizing your closet and drawers into categories. Hang all jackets together, all pants together, all skirts together, and so on. Arrange the items by color families. Separate suit jackets, skirts, and pants so that you can coordinate them with other separates in your wardrobe. Sweaters should not be hung on a hanger but folded. Hanging a sweater causes it to stretch. Hangers can also cause snags. Skirts and pants should be hung on pant hangers to keep wrinkles to a minimum. If you do not have pant hangers, a plastic hanger will work. Simply fold in half and place on hanger. Keeping your clothes organized by season, color, and category, helps make matching outfits easier. Putting your clothes back into your closet and drawers and re-organizing as you go, will also help you see combinations you never thought of wearing before.

Finally, after organizing your closet and drawers, make a list of what you have in your wardrobe and establish what you need to purchase on a separate list. This will help you determine without a doubt what you own in your wardrobe and what you will need to purchase. Instead of wasting time and energy shopping for items you do not need, you will be able to shop and select items that will complement your wardrobe. Learning how to shop wisely saves you time and money, and you will most likely end up coming home with the right item.

Color

Have you ever noticed how many different colors there are on the earth? God is so creative and colorful. He has created all the wonderful colors that we see each day. God did a wonderful and brilliant job expressing himself with color, and you too can express yourself by the colors you choose to wear. For example, if you want to look important and make a statement, red would be your color. If you want to look less noticeable yet make a statement, then a shade of pink or pastel would be your color. Color does play an important role in your wardrobe and in your make-up bag.

Do you look in your closet and find the same old colors? Do you find yourself buying neutral colors like black, white, or brown when you go shopping? Most likely your answer would be yes. It takes a very confident woman to wear colors that stand out.

Don't be afraid of color. Color can be a starting point in your wardrobe planning, as well as having a strong effect on your feelings and your personality. Visit your local cosmetic counter to help determine what colors would look best on you. You can also locate a local stylist to help you determine what colors and styles would work best for your lifestyle and body type. There is also a lot of information on the Internet that can help you.

A Closer Look at Accessories

When wearing an outfit, you want to look your best from crown to toe. Accessories are a great way to personalize your look. Accessories include a number of things besides what you find in your jewelry box. Accessories include items like your shoes, hosiery, socks, scarves, hair accessories, purses and bags, gloves, and sunglasses. There are many things you can add to an outfit to accessorize it. Accessorizes are just as important as your clothing items. Clean clothes and clean accessories go together. Look at your accessories and answer these questions. Does my jewelry sparkle and look clean? Are my shoes polished? Are my handbags clean and free from dirt and scuffs? Do my stockings have holes or runners? Are my hair clips and accessories clean and not broken? Are my glasses free from fingerprints and dirt, are they broken or chipped? The next time you are ready to accessorize, take a closer look and make sure they are in tip-top shape before wearing them.

How to Keep Great Looking Accessories

Keep your delicate hosiery in a large, zip-lock bag to avoid finding unwanted snags.

Keep your matching earrings together on an earring tree, placed neatly in a jewelry box lined with felt, or sorted by color in zip-lock snack bags.

Keep your necklaces free from tangles by simply hanging them on a hook or laying them flat in a jewelry box that is stationary.

Keep your hair accessories neatly organized by placing them by style in a drawer organizer or keep them separated in zip-lock bags.

Keep purses and handbags hung on a hook or placed neatly on a shelf rather than throwing them into a drawer or onto the floor.

Keep your shoes on a shoe rack and up off the floor or store them in shoeboxes when not in use.

Keep your shoes and boots polished and free from scuffs by polishing them after each wear. Remove scuffs by using a Mr. Clean eraser pad.

Keep your belts hung neatly by color on a belt rack. If you do not have a belt rack simply, hang them on a hanger and buckle belt to secure.

Keep your scarves hanging in your closet so you can easily match with your wardrobe. Store them on a hanger and tie to hanger to secure.

Shoe Shining Tips

Leather Shoes

First, wipe off any dirt with a dampened sponge or cloth and scrape off any dried on mud. Secondly, clean shoe with a saddle soap. Wipe off any excess lather and rub with a clean dry cloth. Then, shine shoes by applying wax or polish. Use neutral polish or polish that matches your leather. Apply wax or polish with a dry soft cloth or sock. Wax helps keep leather shoes soft and makes them last longer. Finish off your shine by rubbing your shoes with a soft cloth or brush.

Fabric, Canvas, or Suede Shoes

Throw into washing machine and wash in cold water. Let air dry. To treat spots, make a paste from your powdered laundry detergent and apply to stained area, let set overnight and wash.

Plastic Shoes

To remove black scuffmarks, use a Mr. Clean eraser pad, or simply wash them off with warm soapy water.

What Not to Wear

There is a popular TV show called "What Not to Wear." This shows puts a surprised person on the spot about the way they dress. They then invite them to enjoy a week of shopping and fashion consultations away from home. In the process, the person gets a new wardrobe, a new hair style, a new make-up look, and a boost of self-confidence. However, not everyone gets the opportunity to be on a show like this. Women are always looking for the perfect outfit and things that will help her look her best. But true beauty is not all about wearing the perfect fitting clothes, shoes, and the sporting the perfect haircut; there are other things that should be worn to enhance your outward beauty. Beauty is found in the total package, from crown to toe, and from heart to soul. True beauty comes from the attitude of the heart. Here are some things the Bible tells us not to wear:

A negative attitude, envy, anger, grumpiness, bitterness, a lying tongue, ungratefulness, sadness, a frown, unkindness, disrespect, gossip, selfishness, rudeness, fear, jealousy, a filthy mouth, pride.

What to Wear

happiness, love, gratefulness, kindness, thoughtfulness, garment of praise, righteousness, long suffering, patience, goodness, faith, godliness, gentleness, compassion, wisdom, forgiveness, obedience, confidence, truth, a smile.

How to Look Like a Princess

Always wear a smile

Use eye contact

Stand-up straight

Hold your chin up and your shoulders back

Walk with confidence

Don't hide behind your hair or make-up

Always look your best from crown to toe

Keep your nervous habits to yourself, (i.e. fidgeting, biting nails, playing with your hair, swinging your foot)

Be grateful for any compliments you may receive

How to Look Like a Princess Cont.

Let Jesus shine through you

Walk in love

Have respect for others feelings

Speak to everyone

Call people by their name

Be friendly and helpful

Be cordial

Be generous with your praise and be cautious with your criticism

Avoid sarcastic remarks

Be interested in the affairs of others

Be ready to help without being asked

Always have a kind word to say

Keep your opinions and attitudes to yourself

Practice good manners

Practice good posture

Keep your feet far from evil

Walk in the fruit of the spirit

Walk in your God-given authority

Be faithful in your commitments

Never speak out of turn

Always be ready to share the gospel

Princess Wardrobe Tips

Keep your clothes neat and clean.

Keep your shoes polished and clean by washing them often. Keep a Mr. Clean erase pad on hand for stubborn stains.

If it needs to be mended—mend before wearing it.

Keep your delicate stockings in a zip lock bag.

Keep your accessories clean, including your handbags and hair bows.

Wash out stains as soon as they happen.

Blouses should not be any lower than four fingers width down from the collarbone.

When wearing low-rise jeans, make sure your undies are low-rise as well.

Jeans should be able to be pulled away from the leg easily.

Your body is the temple of the Holy Spirit—keep it clean and neat.

Express yourself in a modest and attractive way.

Instead of keeping up with the fashions and fads—find what fits your lifestyle and wear it with confidence.

Don't wear something that would cause someone to stumble.

God looks at the appearance of your heart. How is it dressed?

All About Me

This worksheet will help you take a closer look at who you are. On a separate sheet of paper, answer the following questions.

1. What is the color of your hair?

2. What is the color of your eyes?

3. How much do you weigh and what is your ideal weight?

4. How tall are you and do you like your height?

5. Measure your bust, waist, and hips, and comment on the way you feel about each one.

6. How do you feel about your overall appearance?

7. What areas can of your life can you improve and how can you go about improving them?

8. Does your appearance affect the way you feel about yourself and the way you treat others?

9. What color is your skin?

10. Do you like the color of skin God has given you? Why or why not?
_____
_____

11. How would you describe the overall appearance of your skin?
_____
_____

12. What can you do to improve the appearance of your skin?
_____
_____

13. How would you describe your teeth?
_____

14. How can you improve the appearance of your teeth?
_____
_____

15. Do you like the way you laugh, the sound of your voice, and your personality?
_____
_____

16. Choose adjectives that best describe your personality.
_____
_____

17. How can you enhance and embrace your personality?
_____
_____

18. Do you like what you see when you look in the mirror? Why or why not?
_____
_____
_____

The reason for these questions is to help you understand how you feel about yourself. How will you understand something until you first study it? Your answers will help you understand who you are. There are many things that can be changed about your appearance, but there are also many that cannot be changed. That is, unless you become someone you are not. The fact is, you are the way God created you to be. You are a unique, divine design. God has specifically designed and fashioned you to fit your body.

Do not be afraid or resentful of the reflection you see in the mirror. Choose to love that person you see and know in your heart that you were created with the ideas of God. Love yourself no matter what the mirror reflects back to you. It is all about you. Love your height, love your personality, love your teeth, love the way your laugh sounds, love your smile, love the way you look. After all, God loved you first[1] so that you could love yourself in return. Be happy with who you are and rejoice in everything about you.

Princess Bible Verse

Romans 12:1-2 NKJV

"I beseech you therefore, brethren, by the mercies of God, that you present your bodies a living sacrifice, holy, acceptable to God, which is your reasonable service. And do not be conformed to this world, but be transformed by the renewing of your mind, that you may prove what is that good and acceptable and perfect will of God."

👑 Princess Beauty Tips

A princess keeps her clothes hung on clothes hangers to keep them nice and neat. Although there will be many hang-ups in life, God will never leave you hanging by yourself. He will always be there to help keep you nice and neat.

👑 Princess Confessions

I will choose to wear clothes that will not be misleading to others and will use wisdom in my fashion statements.

👑 Princess Prayer

Lord, in a world where fashion seems to matter it is easy to be caught up in the wrong things. I repent and ask for your forgiveness for not putting your ideas first in my life when it comes to the way I dress. I ask your help to remove those things from my life which are not pleasing in your sight. In Jesus' name, Amen.

👑 Princess Challenge

Get rid of clothes that are too revealing, throw out clothes that are too small, and every time you buy a new item for your closet, give one away.

👑 Princess Crown Thought

The clothes you wear are a representation of who you are. Wearing low fitting jeans or tops doesn't send the right message of a daughter of God.

👑 Princess Journaling Assignment

Do I dress according to the ideals of God, or am I dressing to fit the ideals of the world? How can I improve the way I dress? Does the way I choose to dress causing someone to stumble? Am I modest in my apparel? How can I do better?

Write Your Own Prayer:

Poise

Lisa Delmedico Harris

Chapter 12

God and Your Posture

Did you know there is an art to standing, sitting, and walking? Good posture can show self-confidence and can speak a lot about how you feel about yourself to others. Good posture starts by recognizing that you may have a bad posture habit. In this chapter, you will learn the right and wrong ways of good posture. The Bible is full of many scriptures that teach us the proper way to walk, talk, sit, dress, behave, and live. For example, Romans 13:13 tells us to walk properly, and not in lewdness, lust, strife or envy. God expects you to walk with confidence, in righteousness, in peace, and in his commandments and ordinances. If you walk in God's ways it will help keep you from slouching. As Christians, we have become sloppy and slouchy. We have given into the world's ways and views of how we are to live our lives. We have gotten away from the true values and instructions of the word of God. After all, the word of God is living and powerful, and the world of living is dead to sin. We have compromised to the world system about how we are to act, dress, sit, walk, talk, eat, and serve God. You will find numerous times in the word of God that the righteous shall have life and all that pertains to it. Proverbs 11:21 says, "the uncompromisingly righteous shall be delivered." God's standards are higher than the world's standards. In fact, the world has no standards at all, just methods and myths on how you are to live.

We have become sloppy and slouchy Christians by the way we blend in with the social norm and mix in with society. We are to stand out in a world that needs us the most. We should be walking, talking, and living like the royalty we are. We are a chosen people, a peculiar people, and God has instructed us to stand out in a crowd. Instead of standing out, we are blending in with what everyone else is doing. We have picked the world's philosophy of anything goes. God has called us out, set us apart, and recreated us in his image. His image should reflect something different and unique.

One way we have blended in with society is in the way we dress. Just because a friend is wearing it and showing it, doesn't mean you have to do the same. The fashion industry does a great job showing off nudity in creative ways and most of those ways should be left on the runway. Choose to raise your standards to meet the expectations of God's word and dress accordingly and respectfully.

We no longer work to look our best, but instead we slouch to convenience and depend on wonder drugs and diet pills to do the work for us. Having good posture, like anything else, takes work and effort. Do not expect to take a pill that can cure your slouching, instead rely on your own efforts to stand up and to stand out.

We have become slouchy and sloppy in the way we eat and treat ourselves. We no longer care about our bodies from the inside out. If you are not at your ideal weight, put God into your diet plan. He will help and teach you on how to take care of yourself. Respect yourself and take pride in the way you look. Your attitude plays an important part in the way you look and feel. If you do not feel good on the inside, you are not going to care about what you look like on the outside. On the other hand, you may go to the other extreme and try to cover-up the way you feel on the inside by painting up and dressing up the outside. Do not slouch to your past. Lay your past behind you and press toward the mark of the high calling in Christ Jesus.[1] Sin, and your past will cause you to have poor posture. Let it go, and give it to God. You don't need the extra weight to carry around with you. You will only end up with back pains.

We have slouched in our relationship with our Lord and Savior Jesus. He is the maker of the universe, creator of everything, including you. Do not allow your shoulders to shrug with your relationship with him. Spend time in fellowship with him every day. Stay in a constant attitude of prayer, acknowledge him in all your ways, read his word, and cast your cares and thoughts on him daily. Don't become so busy that you forget the most important friend you will ever have in your life. Don't forget that he needs your attention and your affection. The perfect way to practice good posture is to stand with your arms outstretched and your hands reaching toward the sky, praising and giving thanks unto the Lord.

Poise begins with your investment in liking yourself and increases as you gain self-confidence. Loving yourself is the key factor in having great posture. When you feel great about yourself and your confidence is on the high, you cannot help but stand upright. It is that Princess Power, the power of the love of Jesus in your life, helping you love yourself and others around you. Without it, you cannot have great posture. Without love, nothing works. Love yourself, value yourself, and respect yourself. Give yourself a hug and say aloud in front of a mirror, "I am good! I can stand up and stand tall in Christ Jesus!" His love should dwell in you so much that it overflows onto others and be evident in the way you see and treat yourself. Without love, you can never have true self-confidence, self-esteem, correct posture, or have a healthy sense of personal value.

We have also become sloppy and slouchy in the way we dress and present ourselves to others. First impressions do matter, although you may not think anyone around you is watching, there are many who watch you every day. You may not ever meet them or ever know who they are. Your impression is what you leave behind. Take care of your body by eating healthy, exercising and bathing regularly, practicing personal grooming habits, good manners, and dressing modestly. You can allow yourself to be a stumbling block in the lives of others who may be watching if you do not pay close attention to the things in your life. You are a representation of Jesus the Lord.

Out of all the ways we have become sloppy and slouchy, slouching spiritually is the worst posture habit of them all. Sadly to say, the majority of born-again believers have not fully experienced the meaning of "having correct posture in Christ." Correct posture in Christ means that we understand the power and position we have in him. God has given us everything that pertains to life and godliness.[2] We have been given authority over the powers of darkness and all that it brings.[3] We have been given power through the blood of Jesus, through the word of God, and by his powerful name. We have been given dominion on this earth.[4] Sickness and diseases are under our feet, poverty is under our feet, lack is under our feet, and the entire curse found in Deuteronomy 28 is under our feet. We have been redeemed from the curse according to Galatians 3:13. Stand up straight in your God-given posture through Jesus Christ. You are seated in heavenly places and have been raised up with him. [5] You are royalty; sit, stand, walk, talk, and act like the king's daughter you are. Do not slouch or become sloppy in any way. God is depending on you to stand-up straight so you can run the race he has prearranged for you to run.

Correct Posture

Creating good posture will involve forming new habits. Good posture starts by recognizing how your posture is now. To determine how your posture is now, first stand face forward in front of a full-length mirror, and examine the position of your head, your shoulders, and your tummy. Second, view your posture from a side angle. Imagine a straight line running down the middle of the mirror from top to bottom. For a guide, you can, draw a line with an erasable marker down the center of the mirror, running from top to bottom. Position yourself sideways in front of the mirror. The line should run, starting at the top, from the center of your ear, down to the center of your shoulder, elbow, hip, thigh, knee, and ankle area. Examine the position of your head, your shoulders, and your tummy using the straight line. Take a mental note of the things you see that don't line-up with the drawn or imaginary line. For example, my shoulders are slouching slightly forward. Correct posture should be measured by imagining a string pulling you upward from the top of your head just like a puppet on a string.

Your body tells a lot about who you are. Speak good words with your body language whether you are sitting, standing, or walking. Post notes on your bathroom mirror that will help remind you to stand tall and have good posture. Ask someone to help you analyze your posture. They may notice things abut your posture that you cannot see. Creating good posture habits will take time, work, and practice, but it will help you improve if you are willing. Keep your posture on your mind and continually remind yourself to stand up straight and tall. By continually reminding yourself of good posture habits, you will soon start to notice a change in the way you look and feel. Others will take notice as well. Bad posture not only looks unprofessional and appears sloppy, but it is also bad for your health.

Art of Walking

Walking should be controlled and performed gracefully. For example, clomping your way down the hall at school or work does not show control or grace. Walking gracefully means walking with your chin up, shoulders square, tummy tucked in, and with smooth, short steps. Also make sure your arms glide by your side gracefully. A graceful and controlled walk says, look at me—I am full of confidence.

Art of Sitting

Sitting is an important art to learn. The proper way to sit in a chair is really quite easy when you remember these important rules. When approaching a chair, don't let your bottom hunt for the chair. Instead, use your hands, legs and eyes. Keep your eye on the chair so you don't turn around and hit the floor. Keep your back straight, turn and stand in front of it so that the back of your calf muscle touches the edge. Once the back of your leg is touching, keep your body straight from the waist up and bend only your knees to sit down. Use your legs and hands to push yourself back into the chair. In some cases, like job interviews, choose to sit on the edge of your chair rather than pushing yourself all the way to the back. Cross your legs at your ankles and lay your hands on top of one another in your lap gracefully. If you are not very tall and your feet cannot touch the floor, scoot forward in the chair so that the bend of your leg reaches the edge. You can choose to use the arm of the chair for a backrest. The key to looking great in a chair is to relax, sit up straight, and show confidence.

Art of Stooping

Stooping can be very embarrassing, not to mention revealing. When stooping, remember to bend at the knee and keep your back straight; it doesn't look very graceful to bend over from the waist to pick something up. Approach the object in the floor and stand in front of it. Stoop down by bending your knees while keeping your back and upper body straight. Drop down one knee, for balance, and reach for the object. To raise up gracefully, again keep upper body straight and use your feet and legs to push yourself up.

Art of Carrying

Unbelievably as it may sound, there is even an art to carrying books or other items. Carrying your books high on the hipbone and with good posture is the key. Avoid carrying heavy amounts of weight at one time. If your load is heavy, switch arms and shoulders to avoid tugging on just one shoulder.

Art of Entering and Exiting a Room

If you are entering a room without having to open or close a door, remember to walk with good posture and wear a smile. Keep your eyes focused on were you are going and keep your chin up. If you are entering a room where you have to open and close a door, simply open the door, step into the room, then switch hands to close the door behind you. Never turn and face the door to close it, instead keep your body facing forward so that you never turn your back to the people inside.

Art of Getting In and Out of a Car

When getting into a car, let your rear lead you in and let your feet follow. Bring your feet in together by keeping your knees together as much as possible. Use this technique especially if you are wearing a skirt or dress. Use good judgment when getting into any vehicle. Avoid slouching yourself into the car and ducking your head in first. To get out of a car, slide your feet over to the outside while keeping your ankles together and place both feet on the ground. Scoot up to the edge and push yourself up and out using legs and arms.

Art of Walking Up and Down Stairways

Walking up stairways can be tricky and dangerous. Always approach the stairs by first observing the full stairway you are about to ascend or descend. Pause before the staircase, and look up or down before taking the first step. Place the first foot forward firmly on the first step. Keep your body straight and do not look around. Focus on the stairs you are walking. Look ahead, and not down. With one foot firmly on the step, lift the other foot and place onto the next step. Continue until you have reached the top or bottom. Keep your toes pointed straight ahead and your knees close together. Move your body in a rhythmic motion up or down the staircase. Grip the stair handrail and keep your eyes focused on where you are going. Don't stomp or bounce your way up or down the staircase.

Princess Posture Tips

Your body language says a lot about who you are.

Always stand up straight and tall by keeping your shoulders rolled back.

When standing, walking, or sitting, imagine an invisible string attached to the top of your head pulling you upward.

When walking, keep your chin up and your eyes focused on where you are going.

Practice good posture no matter where you are.

There is always someone watching you. Set a good example for others to follow.

Good posture takes practice.

When getting in and out of a car, make sure you keep your legs close together, especially when you are wearing a dress.

Sit up straight and tall in your chair with your hands pleasantly placed in your lap.

When stooping to the floor, always bend at your knees and keep your back straight.

A princess always takes notice of how she enters and exits a room.

A princess never slouches, and always walks with a smile.

When carrying heavy books or bags, remember to switch arms to lighten the weight.

You are full of potential, abilities, gifts, and talents.

The Way Jesus Walked

Jesus walked this earth as a man. Jesus practiced good posture no matter where he was or what he was doing. When studying the life of Jesus, we will find that he walked in perfect time with perfect posture. The Bible says in I John 2:6, "He who says he abides in him ought [as a personal debt] to walk and conduct himself in the same way in which he walked and conducted himself." How do we know how Jesus walked while he was on this earth? We study his life and learn from it.

If we say we are Christians and proclaim we are children of God, then we should learn how a child of God should walk. If we all were to take etiquette lessons from the Word of God, we would learn more about the importance of having good posture and good manners, and more about how we can walk in the perfect ways of God. Don't just proclaim to be a Christian, walk like one, act like one, be one.

Jesus walked without sin.	I John 3:9
Jesus walked in love.	John 4:16
Jesus walked in the truth.	Psalm 26:3
Jesus walked in peace	Romans 5:1, Is 26:3
Jesus walked in the anointing.	Isaiah 61:1
Jesus walked in mercy.	Psalm 103:17
Jesus walked in grace.	Psalm 84:11
Jesus walked in wisdom.	James 1:5
Jesus walked in compassion.	Luke 20:30
Jesus walked in authority and power.	Philippians 2:9-11
Jesus walked in the ways and in the laws of God.	Luke 2:49
Jesus walked in freedom.	Galatians l 5:1, John 8:31
Jesus walked in prayer.	Philippians 4:6, Ephesians 6:18

The Way Jesus Walked Cont.

Jesus walked in the fruits of the spirit.	Galatians 5:22, 23
Jesus walked in forgiveness.	I John 1: 9
Jesus walked in perfection.	Hebrews 5:9
Jesus walked in strength.	Psalm 73:26
Jesus walked in hope and in a future.	Jeremiah 29:11
Jesus walked in health and healing.	Isaiah 53:4, 5
Jesus walked in the ways of his Father.	Luke 2:49

♛ Princess Bible Verse

1 John 2:6

"He who says he abides in him ought himself also to walk just as he walked."

👑 Princess Beauty Tips

A throne is a great way for a princess to remember how to use good posture. The back of the throne is straight and tall and helps keep it upright. When using good posture, keep your back straight, stand tall, and walk upright. God has raised you up with Jesus and seated you in heavenly places at the right side of the Father.

👑 Princess Confessions

I will walk in the ways of the Lord and follow him all the days of my life.

👑 Princess Prayer

Lord, teach me to understand where I am seated in Christ Jesus and what posture in you really means. Help me to also understand my authority on this earth given to me through the works of Christ Jesus. Teach me how to walk in your ways always. In Jesus' name, Amen.

👑 Princess Challenge

Make an effort to roll your shoulders back and walk with your chin up, sit up straighter in your chair, and make a difference in your posture.

👑 Princess Crown Thought

The worst posture you can have is to sit down and give up. There is victory in standing and never giving up.

👑 Princess Journaling Assignment

Am you living your life in a way that is pleasing in the sight of the Lord? Are you kind to others? Do you present yourself well in front of others? Are you using good posture? Are you allowing the burdens of this life to cause you to slouch? Do you trust in the Lord with all your heart, soul, mind, and strength? Is your walk leading others to Christ?

_____

_____

_____

_____

_____

_____

_____

_____

_____

_____

_____

_____

_____

_____

_____

_____

_____

Write Your Own Prayer:

Chapter 13

God and Your Confidence

Self-confidence is being confident in yourself and your abilities. It's believing in yourself and not allowing fears to intimidate you. It's knowing who you are: your weakness, and your strengths. You have to believe in yourself. However, self-confidence is more than just believing in yourself; self-confidence is also knowing what God thinks of you. Knowing God's thoughts helps build self-confidence and keeps you strong. Most people lack self-confidence and the courage to believe in their abilities and who they are. You are not born with self-confidence, it is instilled in you through your own mindset and beliefs. It is something that develops with time and maturity. Once you start believing in yourself, you can be successful in whatever you set your mind to do. If you believe in yourself, you can unleash the potential for greatness to operate in your life. Without first believing in yourself and having hope to continue on, you will not have the desire to seek greatness.

Hope deferred will make the heart sick.[1] If you do not have hope in yourself and for the future, then you will be unhappy and never accomplish the great things God has planned for you to do. Having hope will carry you through life, and without it, you will become sick in your heart or your mind, will, and emotions. Hope motivates and tells you to keep going and pressing on toward your goals. Hope helps you to keep a positive outlook. When others are weak and weary around you, you will be able to lift them up by the hope and confidence that lives in you. Many people lack self-confidence and hope. Jesus Christ is the author of hope. He is the only who can instill hope and confidence.

The word of God has a lot to say about confidence.

"Do not, therefore, fling away your fearless confidence, for it carries a great and glorious compensation of reward. For you have need of steadfast patience and endurance, so that you may perform and fully accomplish the will of God, and thus receive and carry away [and enjoy to the full] what is promise."
Hebrews 10:35-36

Don't throw away your confidence. You will be richly rewarded when you stand in it. You will need a strong self-confidence to help you accomplish the plans God has made for you. There will be times when failure will try to rob you of your confidence, but remember to stand strong and be steadfast. God's plan will also include you stepping out of your comfort zone and doing things you have never done before. Maybe you are frightened to stand and speak in front of a crowd, or maybe you are frightened to pursue the dreams of your heart. Whatever the situation, God has given you his confidence to help you continue on even whenever it seems too difficult.

Don't let failure or fear rob you of what God has in store. Many people give up when they lose confidence in themselves and when things get too tough. However, with patience and endurance God says you can do it and you will fully accomplish the will of God for your life. A strong confidence comes from renewing your old thought patterns and replacing with new and positive ones.

Most problems in life start when you give up and lose your confidence. Your joy and strength disappear when there is no hope. For the joy of the Lord is your strength.[2] Fear will steal your strength, and fear is only false evidence appearing real. Don't let fear have a place in your life and rob everything God has for you. Without confidence, you will never experience true joy and peace. Your confidence in Christ and knowing who you are in him will determine your level of peace, joy, and happiness. Search the Bible to find those scriptures that say "in him," "in whom," and "in Christ." These phrases mean you! You are entitled to the blessings of God.

When you don't have confidence in yourself through Jesus Christ, you grieve the Holy Spirit. He cannot bring those things to pass which God has promised to you if you allow confidence to lie dormant in your soul. The Holy Spirit can hardly wait for you to unleash the righteousness of God in your life through confidence. You are full of great potential, special gifts, and abilities. Only God could place those wonderful qualities in you. You have been given these wonderful attributes of God to help you accomplish God's will for your life.

 Don't be afraid of the things you are not able to do; instead, concentrate on those things that you are good at. Pursue your talents and abilities. Don't sit on your talents and do nothing with them. Sharpen them and perfect them. Having confidence in your talents and abilities will help you do great and mighty things for the kingdom of God. God uses people to accomplish his will on this earth, and you are a part of his plan. Be firm, unshakeable, and balanced in your self-confidence. God needs you.

If you don't let the confidence in Christ Jesus rule and reign in your heart, you will be leaving a door wide open for the devil to come into your life. When he comes, he will bring with him weapons of mass destruction like torment, self-hatred, shame, and, fear. He will find any way to kill, steal, and destroy you and your future. The devil will do anything he can to sabotage your self-esteem and rob you of your confidence. He does not want you to develop those God-given assets that were put in you at birth.

The devil knows what you are capable of with Jesus in your life. He knows that you are a divine seed sowed into this world to do great things for the kingdom of God. Princess, don't let the devil your enemy, rob you of your self-confidence and self-esteem. Put your confidence in Jesus and let him use you in great and mighty ways. You can do all things through Christ Jesus who gives you the strength.[3]

Bible Study on Confidence

"It is better to trust and take refuge in the Lord than to put confidence in man". Psalm 118:8

"For we (Christians) are the true circumcision, who worship God in spirit and by the Spirit of God and exult and glory and pride ourselves in Jesus Christ, and put no confidence or dependence (on what we are) in the flesh and on outward privileges and physical advantages and external appearances." Philippians 3:3

"For the Lord shall be your confidence, firm and strong, and shall keep your foot from being caught [in a trap or some hidden danger].". Proverbs 3:26

"In the reverent and worshipful fear of the Lord there is strong confidence, and his children shall always have a place of refuge". Proverbs 14:26

"For we have become partakers of Christ if we hold the beginning of our confidence steadfast to the end." Hebrews 3:14 NKJV

"In whom, because of our faith in him, we dare to have the boldness (courage and confidence) or free access (an unreserved approach to God with freedom and without fear)." Ephesians 3:12

"Do not, therefore, fling away your fearless confidence, for it carries a great and glorious compensation of reward." Hebrews 10:35

"And now, little children, abide (live, remain permanently) in him, so that when he is made visible, we may have and enjoy perfect confidence (boldness, assurance) and not be ashamed and shrink from him at his coming." 1 John 2:28

"And, beloved, if our consciences (our hearts) do not accuse us [if they do not make us feel guilty and condemn us], we have confidence (complete assurance and boldness) before God, and we receive from him whatever we ask, because we [watchfully] obey his orders [observe his suggestions and injunctions, follow his plan for us] and [habitually] practice what is pleasing to him." 1 John 3:21

"And this is the confidence (the assurance, the privilege of boldness) which we have in him: [we are sure] that if we ask anything (make any request) according to his will (in agreement with his own plan), he listens to and hears us." 1 John 5:14

Princess Bible Verse

Philippians 3:3

"For we (Christians) are the true circumcision, who worship God in spirit and by the Spirit of God and exult and glory and pride ourselves in Jesus Christ, and put no confidence or dependence (on what we are) in the flesh and on outward privileges and physical advantages and external appearances."

Princess Beauty Tips

A toothbrush is a tool a princess uses to improve the appearance of her smile. She uses it to brush away the dullness on her teeth. Self-confidence is a lot like a toothbrush. Self-confidence helps put a beautiful smile on your face. When you have confidence and know who you are in Christ, then the bristles of life will only help improve your appearance and cause your confidence to shine.

Princess Confessions

I will have confidence in God and in myself. I will not put my confidence in my outward privileges and physical advantages, but only in those things that are everlasting.

Princess Prayer

Lord, I put my confidence in you and pray that you will help me to remain in it. I praise you that you have made available to me the confidence I need to be successful and happy in this life. I thank you for all you have done for me. I have confidence in knowing that you have given me life, hope, and a future. I praise the name of Jesus in which my confidence is found. I pray you will help me to walk and talk in your confidence and strength. Through your strength I am able to act upon the confidence you have freely given to me. Thank you for imparting in me the wonderful power of your Spirit. In Jesus' name, Amen.

Princess Challenge

Fear is just a feeling and can only have an influence over you if you give in to it. Cast down your thoughts and feeling of fear and step out and try something new. Even if you fail, at least you had the courage to try.

Princess Crown Thought

God Confidence will take you to heights you never thought you could reach.

Princess Journaling Assignment

Make a list of things you would like to do but are afraid of trying. What are your strengths and weaknesses? What are your talents and natural abilities? Do you let fear keep you from stepping out of your comfort zone? When you step out of this zone it requires trust. Do you trust in the Lord? Write the definition of trust.

Write Your Own Prayer:

Chapter 14

God and Your Attitude

Attitude is the posture of the body in connection with an action or mood. It manages the way we act, feel, and think. Attitude is your mindset in motion. We all have been given the opportunity of choice. We have the choice to have a good attitude or to have a bad attitude. A good attitude sees the good in everything and is ready to help in all situations. A good attitude will help you to live in peace and in harmony with others. God walked this earth as a man in with a good attitude. He was tempted in every way the Bible says, but he chose to resist temptation and stand in the ways of God. Sometimes it may seem life has treated you unfairly, and from those unfair times you have developed a bad attitude or mindset. In our society, "I don't care" is a common way to live. But you don't have to live in misery and despair. Although life doesn't always treat you kindly, you can chose to look at it with a positive outlook and with a good attitude. God has bought you with a price and has given you all things that pertain to life and godliness. Having a good attitude is a start to godliness.

A person with a good attitude or outlook on life is often referred to as an optimistic person. An optimistic person sees the good in every situation and lives by faith. A person with an optimistic mindset is also someone who speaks good words and thinks good thoughts. A person with a bad attitude or outlook on life is just the opposite and is referred to as a pessimist. A pessimistic person sees the bad in every situation and lives in fear. A pessimistic person's mouth is filled with words of fear and disappointment. God wants you to be an optimistic person. The person of faith who always looks to him in every situation and doesn't let the heaviness of life weigh them down.

God tells us in Philippians 4:8 what to think about so we can stay in a positive mindset. If there were no guidelines for our thoughts, then our mind would run wild with fear and negativity. Our mind is a constant battlefield of thoughts. But we have the power within us to tame those thoughts and to cast them down.

"For the weapons of our warfare are not carnal but mighty in God for pulling down strongholds, casting down arguments and every high thing that exalts itself against the knowledge of God, bringing every thought into captivity to the obedience of Christ."

II Corinthians 10:4-5

It is our responsibility to bring every thought into captivity. In others words, we are to stop the evil thoughts in our mind before they become strongholds in our life. We are to stop bad attitudes before they take root and become mindsets. It is also up to us to conform our thinking and transform our minds to what the Bible says. If you are not reading the Bible and filling your mind with good thoughts of wisdom and strength then you will not be stable in all your ways. Establishing a good attitude will take dedication to being attentive to your thoughts and feelings and not letting them get the best of you. Cast your cares on the Lord and let him help you establish a good attitude and develop a positive outlook.

Matthew 7:16 says you will know a person by their fruits. A person with a good attitude will show good fruit in their life, like the fruit of kindness, love, and thankfulness. A person with a bad attitude will show just the opposite. What is your life displaying? Are you showing good fruit with the way you choose to behave with your attitude?

If your attitude is in need of repair, rely on Jesus and the light of his word to help you grow and mature your character and attitude. Be dedicated to your thoughts by making sure they are in line with the word of God and Philippians 4:8 and you will see an improvement in your attitude. Take this simple attitude test to see if your attitude is in tune with God.

The Attitude Test

Answer these questions to learn more about your attitude and how it is affecting your life and relationships.

Do you find fault in everything around you, people, situations, environment, school, work, or society? Yes or No. Explain.

_____

_____

Do you see the bad in everything? Explain.

_____

_____

Do you get along well with others, or do you let your opinions hinder your relationships? Yes or No. Explain.

_____

_____

Do your friends have an influence on your attitude? Yes or No. Explain.

_____

_____

Does your attitude stand between you and someone you love? Yes or No. Explain.

_____

_____

Does your attitude affect the way you dress and take care of yourself? Yes or No. Explain.

_____
_____

Are your thoughts filled with love and life, or are they filled with thoughts of gloom and despair? Yes or No. Explain.

_____
_____

How would you describe your attitude? Positive (optimistic) or Negative (pessimistic). Explain.

_____
_____

Does your attitude determine your decisions? Yes or No. Explain.

_____
_____

Does your attitude get in the way of achieving your dreams and goals? Yes or No. Explain.

_____
_____

Does your attitude affect the way you respond to authority? Yes or No. Explain.

_____
_____

The fact is we are all in need of an attitude adjustment. No one has a perfect attitude and having a good attitude takes work. Everyone has different outlooks and different opinions—it is what makes the world go around. But the strongest force on the earth is not gravity, it is the power of choice—your will. The will of a person can choose life or death. You are the only one who can choose the outcome of your life. That is why it is important to fill your mind with the word of God. It is the only information that will cause you to be successful in life. God is positive, and his word is full of blessing and goodness.

III John 1:2 tells us God's desire for you is to prosper in all things and be in good health, even as your soul prospers. What does it mean when the Bible says, "even as your soul prospers"? If you stay in the same state of mind and are not willing to change your behaviors and mindsets, then you will never experience victory and enjoy life to the fullest. There are three ways you can use to determine if your soul is prospering: (1) by observing the way you treat others, (2) by the way you treat yourself, and (3) by the way you are progressing in life. If none of these things have changed, then you need to re-evaluate. Change will not come unless you are first willing to change. Change means progress and prosperity. If you keep getting the same results, try something new.

Princess Bible Verse

Philippians 4:8

"...whatever is true, whatever is worthy or reverence and is honorable and seemly, whatever is just, whatever is pure, whatever is lovely and lovable, whatever is kind and winsome and gracious, if there is any virtue and excellence, if there is anything worthy or praise, think on and weigh and take account of these things [fix your minds on them]."

Princess Beauty Tips

A princess can wear a pair of glasses for a wide variety of reasons. She may need them to shade the sun from her eyes or to help her see more clearly. Your attitude can be compared to a pair of glasses. If your attitude is not in focus with the word of God then your vision will be blurred and your outlook on life will be distorted.

Princess Confessions

The Word of God is changing my attitude and outlook on life. I will fix my mind on good thoughts.

Princess Prayer

Lord, help me to become a positive thinker. Sometimes it is hard for me to think on the good when there is so much bad around me. I pray you will continue to guide me and help me along the path of my life. I ask your help to keep the word of God in the midst of my heart and ever before my eyes. Give me the desire to think on those things that are good, pure, noble, lovely, just, and praiseworthy. I want to be pleasing in your sight, and I know that my attitude is an important part of my life. Father, I want to succeed and do the very best I can. Help me to stay positive and not waver in my faith. In Jesus' name, Amen.

Princess Challenge

Be nice to someone today and choose to show them your love through the actions of your attitude.

Princess Crown Thought

Your thoughts will determine your character and develop your attitude so it will be pleasing to God and to those around you.

👑 Princess Journaling Assignment

What are some good and bad things about your attitude? How can you have a better attitude towards others and the things you do? Is your attitude holding back in life? Does it affect your relationships? Is what's in your heart causing you to act the way you do? God knows everything you say and do, are you doing things that are pleasing in His sight?

Write Your Own Prayer:

Chapter 15

God and the Fashion Industry

The fashion industry is one of the largest industries in America and there are many jobs available. For example, you can go to school to be a cosmetologist, a fashion designer, retail store manager, a buyer, or a model. You can study for years learning about fashion history and how it has affected our society. There are numerous opportunities available. God has been involved in the fashion industry, since the beginning of time. In the Garden of Eden, he designed the animal skin garment to protect and cover Adam and Eve before they were expelled from the garden.[1] But that wasn't the first garment in the garden. After Adam and Eve sinned against God they became ashamed and weaved fig leaves together to cover themselves. Their efforts were to try and cover their sin and nakedness before God and today people are still trying to cover their sins.

In the Bible, there are many women documented as seamstresses, clothing store owners, and in the business of selling and buying fashion. Women have played an important role toward the advancement of fashion. The fashion industry has been an important part of history since colonial times. Throughout history, people have used clothing, ornaments, scents, coloring, and decorations to heighten their beauty. They exercised, dieted, and undergone surgery to make their bodies more attractive. No expense was too high and no effort was too great to achieve the ideal beauty.

There were decades when it was proper to have a twenty-four inch waist. To achieve this look, women would bind themselves with tight corsets, so tight that it would affect their health. A law was eventually made to ban corsets from being worn. Today, both men and women spend billions of dollars each year to undergo life-threatening surgeries just for the sake of beauty. They cut, tuck, enhance, lift, and permanently paint things on their bodies to make them feel more beautiful.

There is no doubt our society influences fashion and beauty. We look to prominent men and women, celebrities, supermodels, fashion icons, and pop stars to pattern our fashions. Even women in the 17th century were fascinated with having large breasts and perfect figures. They would go as far as to wear a "bosom helper" which was made of nothing more than paper and glue, or they would tie padding around them to enhance the bust, waist, or rear. The ideal look isn't always blending in with society and what others are doing. The ideal look should be one that you create on your own by choosing to dress according to your personality and built on your belief system. The Bible tells us to dress modestly and with respect for God.

Women are captivated by beauty and looking beautiful, and there is a reason why they feel that way. Lucifer, (Satan's name before the fall from heaven) was a beautiful creature. He was in the presence of God every day. He had all kinds of beautiful stones and jewels that decorated him. However, Satan became conceited in his beauty and splendor and God found sin in his heart.[2] Satan thought he was and could be better than God. Through his own pride of beauty and self-conceitedness, Satan caused himself and others to be kicked out of heaven. The devil is now using the media to portray his idea of beauty in the world. He is using technology and the media to enhance a false deception of beauty. He is using every means available to cause us to focus our attention on only our outward appearance. The devil does not want you to focus inwardly. He knows the potential you have inside, and he doesn't want you to tap into it. If he can distract you with beautiful things and cause you to want them, then he has your mind, will, and emotions. When a person focuses solely on their outward appearance, there is little time left for ambition and life.

The image consultant himself, Jesus Christ, has created us in the image of perfect beauty. Born-again believers with Jesus in their heart and in their life are to feel beautiful and look beautiful all the time. His ways are perfect, and until we have the perfect and beautiful one in our life, we will be deceived by the lies of the enemy and continue to fantasize over unrealistic beauty. True beauty comes from the heart of a person and that heart should be filled with the beauty of Jesus. It is okay to look and feel beautiful. It is okay to be attracted to sparkly things such as diamonds and gold. After all, have you ever considered that your Father in heaven has streets made of gold and gates made of pearls? Why should you desire anything less?

Don't be deceived into thinking you have to meet a specific idea of beauty in order to be accepted. You have already been accepted through the blood of Jesus. Who cares about what others are doing, what others are wearing, or what others are saying? Be the you that you were created to be. Make your own fashion statement.

Modeling

Modeling is a fun and exciting part of the fashion industry. However, modeling is not for everyone. In today's society, girls everywhere have imagined the life of a model. The fact is we have all wanted to be a model or just look like one at some season in our life. But not everyone is called into the world of high fashion and modeling. Before considering the modeling industry, first seek the Lord's wisdom. You should always pray for the perfect will of God in your life and strive to complete that perfect will. Modeling can be a tough, rude, and distorted profession. With the demands of being thin and staying thin, having the right hair, and walking the right walk, modeling can be very stressful on a young woman. In most cases, being a model means:

- Being under the age of twenty.
- Being close to the ideal for facial beauty.
- Being in the top 10% of height.
- Being at the bottom 2% of weight.
- Being at the right place at the right time.

In the world of fashion today, many young women look to fashion magazines and those models in magazines as their role models. Sad to say, but the world of modeling can be a fake and unnatural world to find a positive role model. The fact is, no one can look perfect without a little help. There are many techniques to making models look and appear perfect and flawless on the cover and throughout the pages of magazines. Photography has developed and advanced over time and many new ways of making someone look great have as well. Point and click is the answer to vanishing blemishes, too much fat, small breasts, or even thin lips. Computer made images perfected to deceive the young viewer into thinking they really could look perfect and beautiful is simply just that—a deception.

There are many women who have made successful careers in the modeling and the fashion industry. The key is to find out what God has in store for you and use those gifts and talents for him instead of for the world. Give him glory in whatever you do and seek his judgment over anyone else's. There is nothing wrong with working as a model. Models do many different things. For example, models are used in fashion shows to model clothing. They are used to introduce new hairstyles or make-up trends. They are used to promote products of various kinds. Models are also used for hand, feet, and leg commercials. There are even models that walk around department stores showing new fragrances.

You don't have to be 5"10 and weigh 110 lbs. to get hired for a modeling job. There are many categories of models and different requirements for each. For example, there are petite, junior, missy, plus-size, kid, and high-fashion runway models. The majority of all runway models are approx. 5'9 and up, the taller the better. The reason for the height is the fact that clothing samples are made to fit a size six to eight and someone with long legs. Did you know that the average American women is 154 pounds and is only 5"3?

If you want to learn more about the modeling industry, get involved in your community and sign up for local fashion shows, become a member of a department store fashion board, or contact local business to find out where they get the models they use for their advertisements. In some large cities, you will find production companies that layout department store catalogs and need models to fill the pages. Another advantage of living in a fashion industry city is the fashion markets. During the market months, you can walk through the market place, visit with vendors beforehand, and apply for modeling jobs. Most companies and vendors use the models they find through a modeling agency to fill the majority of modeling jobs. A modeling agency will have connections where you as a free-lance model may not. Although there are many free-lance models that do a great job finding work on their own, but an agent can better market you.

A key tool for the model's tool belt is a portfolio and calling card. The portfolio is a collection of pictures that show your unique style and photogenic ability. It is essential to obtaining modeling jobs. The more styles you can express throughout your portfolio, the better chance you will have at getting a modeling job. The calling card is larger than a postcard and features photos on front and back, along with your name, measurements, and contact information.

Photos should be kept current, and new pictures need to be updated about every three to six months. A portfolio is something you can take on a modeling job interview if you are a freelancer, and a calling card is something your agent sends out to promote your look and experience. Use caution when having photos taken—never take pictures that expose more that you want. Never compromise your biblical standards for anyone. If it means you will lose the job, then you are better off without it. Every decision you make in life will affect the outcome of your success. Make wise choices and pray before making them.

If you sign on with an agent, make sure you understand the full and complete contract. Do not get yourself stuck in a situation that could cost you your reputation or your pocket book. Avoid spending high prices for modeling classes and training. Do your research and ask those who have gone before you. Pageants are a great way to find coaches and advisors. A good agent will not require you to spend any money up front and will never force you into a contract. They will ask for photos to be put into a main agency portfolio. If the agent likes you, they will find you work, and if they do not, they will not.

THE MODEL'S T

The model's T is simply an attractive way to place your feet. It is called a model's T, or model's stance, simply because it is used on the runway. This stance is a great way to place your feet when you are taking pictures or standing in front of people. To stand in a model's T or stance is very simple. Simply imagine standing on a clock face. Place your feet at 10:00 with your right foot pointing at 12. If you are left handed, you can change the position of your feet to match 2:00. In whichever stance you choose, make sure the heel of the foot on 12:00 is placed into the arch of the other.

Pageants

Pageants are another way to work in the fashion industry if you are interested in modeling, acting, or any other kind of promotional work. There are many pageants available to compete. However, pageants may not be what they seem to be in the beautifully printed brochure or magazine article. Pageants, like modeling, can be a rude, distorted, and a highly political world. In some cases you will discover that most of them are rigged. There are many who make a career out of trying to win a local, state, or national title.

You can spend all your money, time, and effort into winning a title that will one day fade away. I will agree that pageants are a great way to build your self-confidence and boost self-esteem, especially if you are a shy person. Most pageants have one overall winner, so your attitude will play an important part in the way you win or lose. For some, there will be more defeats than victories. If you cannot handle defeat then I recommend staying out of the pageant industry. Rule—remember if you lose a competition, don't take it personal. After all, it is only the opinion of three or five judges.

There is more to being a beauty queen than what meets the eye. Sure, the beautiful dress and tiara is enough to work hard for, but wearing that beautiful tiara on your head requires responsibility and commitment. If you are entering a competition, be yourself. Don't be a fake. I have seen many women whom I thought to be very beautiful on the outside, but once their pageant faces were washed away they suddenly became less attractive. Don't hide your true colors behind a mask of fakeness. This is where so many pageant winners get into trouble. They look good on stage in a beautiful gown and rhinestone jewelry, but when it comes to showing off their spirit of excellence and integrity, their beauty seems to fade.

A title of any kind should be worn with integrity, poise, grace, and true beauty. Being a believer is more than just wearing the title sash "Christian," it is a way of life, a way of thinking, a way of doing, a way of acting, a way of walking, and a way of talking. It is a defined lifestyle and should possess the qualities of excellence and greatness. There is nothing wrong with winning titles and pursuing your dreams, but titles alone will not make the difference. It doesn't matter how many titles you can accumulate. In the end, it will be the way others witness your life in play every day that will make the difference.

If you are interested in competing in a pageant, get wisdom. Seek God's direction on which pageants you should enter. There are many pageant systems who are in business to make money. Choose a pageant with a purpose, a pageant where you are free to speak about the goodness of God. A pageant that will allow you to be yourself, express your faith openly, and be all you can be. Don't pursue a title without doing your homework first and even after you have done your homework and decided to compete, you may still find it not to be all it was advertised to be. The world of pageantry is a chance you take. Before considering a pageant, ask yourself, why?

Modeling and Pageant Tips

Pray for wisdom and guidance before deciding to do either.

Take pride in yourself, your values, and your beliefs.

Never compromise for the sake of someone else.

Seek modeling opportunities and pageant titles where you can glorify God in your efforts.

Don't spend a lot of money. Learn the tricks of the trade.

Don't get involved in something you won't be proud of later.

Keep your mind and your body in tiptop shape.

Always dress and act in a professional manner.

Don't slouch to someone else's opinions, know who you are.

Seek modeling opportunities and pageant experiences that will help benefit you in the future.

Always be yourself and don't be fake.

Wear a contagious smile.

Always be kind, considerate, and thoughtful of others.

Pray for those who purposely aggravate you.

Win with dignity and honor

Lose with grace and style.

Wear your title with character and integrity.

Study and show yourself approved in every endeavor.

Be on time, prepared, and ready to go.

Be willing to be helpful.

Thank God for your success and for your failures.

If you are talented, choose pageants and modeling opportunities that will display your abilities.

Never give up on your dreams.

Make sure whatever your hand is set to do, do it with all diligence, wisdom, and direction from God.

Modeling, Pageant, and Fashion Facts

Modeling isn't for everyone.

Modeling takes a lot of self-confidence.

Perfect natural beauty does not exist.

The models you see in magazines are not realistic.

When modeling in a runway show, keep your eyes focused toward the audience, be confident in your step, and smile.

If you are considering entering a pageant, do your homework first.

Entering pageants that offer scholarship monies are a great way to earn money for college.

The modeling and pageant business isn't always glamorous.

There are many great job opportunities for women in the fashion industry like becoming a fashion or interior designer, a fashion or visual merchandiser, a store buyer, or retail store manager.

There is more to being a beauty queen than just wearing a crown.

Models are usually under the age of 20, close to the ideal for facial beauty, in the top 10% of height, at the bottom 2% of weight, at the right place at the right time.

The average American female is 5'3 and 154 lbs.

When doing modeling or pageantry work, never compromise your beliefs for the sake of fame and fortune.

Pursue the imperishable crown of life instead of one that will rust and wither away.

Princess Bible Verse

I Peter 3:3, 4

"Let not yours be the (merely) external adorning with (elaborate) interweaving and knotting of the hair, the wearing of jewelry, or changes of clothes; But let it be the inward adorning and beauty of the hidden person of the heart, with the incorruptible and unfading charm of a gentle and peaceful spirit, which (is not anxious or wrought up, but) is very precious in the sight of God."

Princess Beauty Tips

Clothes are a way we cover our body. Without them we would all be naked. Although clothes hide many things, they cannot hide sin. Princess, don't try to cover you sins with fashion. God sees everything you do, and his blood is the only thing that can cover a multitude of sin.

Princess Confessions

I am a beautiful, vibrant, and talented daughter of God—full of great-untapped potential.

Princess Prayer

Lord, I commit my ways unto you and pray that you will always direct my steps. Help me to make wise decisions and good choices that will affect my life now and in the future. I trust in you Father and pray that you will guide me and satisfy me always. Thank you Lord that you have my life planned from the beginning to the end.

I pray you will make known to me the gifts, talents, and special abilities you have placed in me to prosper and to glorify your name on this earth. In Jesus' name, Amen.

Princess Challenge

Pursue the desire in your heart; you never know what might become of them.

Princess Crown Thought

No matter what you choose to do in life, do it with all your heart, mind, body, and strength.

Princess Journaling Assignment

What kind of things are you interested in pursuing? If you are interested in the fashion industry, write down the reasons why and the jobs you might be interested in trying. Are you a good model for the kingdom of God? Why or why not?

Write Your Own Prayer:

Chapter 15

God and Your Manners

The history of etiquette originated in the 17th century when King Louis the 14th hosted a party of guest in his beautifully manicured courtyard. However, the party didn't go well, and because of it his gardener become very upset. The guests were very disrespectful of the king's property by walking on the grass, picking the flowers, wading in the fountains, and throwing their trash on the ground. The gardener went to the king with his concerns. They decided to post little signs or tickets around the courtyard instructing the guests to mind their manners. From this idea, etiquette and social graces were introduced into society. In Bible times, the mosaic law was established to form etiquette and social graces among the Israelites.

Etiquette is a french word for "little signs" and what we use to get along with others. Etiquette is a combination of principles and manners. All manners are rooted in three main principles: respect, consideration, and honesty. Saying please turns a demand into a request and shows respect. Saying "thank you" shows appreciation and "you're welcome" acknowledges thank you. The principle in practice is consideration. What you say and how you say it matters. Your tone, your actions, and your expressions are important.

Manners, like a great smile, will match any outfit. Good manners should be a part of your daily routine, just like brushing your teeth and taking a bath. Good manners should be practiced no matter where you are. Being courteous and kind to everyone, including yourself, says a lot about your personality. Your personality also says a lot about who you are. People make character judgments based on the way one handles themselves in social situations.

Always be on your best behavior and use good manners at all times. A person with respect and consideration for others will show and use good manners. Being rude and unkind does not show respect or consideration. God's word tells us many ways to use good manners. In first Peter 3:4 NAS it reads, "Be beautiful inside, in your hearts, with the lasting charm of a gentle and quiet spirit which is so precious to God." God smiles down on you when you are using your best behavior. None of us are perfect and we all mess up from time to time, but God doesn't stop loving us because we make mistakes.[1] He takes those times when we mess up to teach us to be and do better next time. When you do make a mistake, be quick to ask for forgiveness, forget about it, and move on with your life. You have the power to improve your behavior.

Using good manners is a choice you make. When you accepted Jesus as your Savior, something changes. Soon your actions, words, and your appearance will start to be a reflection of him. God expects you to be kind, gentle, and considerate of others. No matter if you are in a classroom learning, sitting at a table eating a meal, or shopping in a mall, he expects you to be on your best behavior.

Love causes you to have good manners. The Bible tells us to love our neighbor as we love ourselves, Matthew 19:19 NKJV. If you have no respect for yourself, you will have no respect for your neighbors. Your neighbors are those people around you including your brothers, sisters, mother, and father. Manners are and expression of love, and love is the greatest expression you can give. Walk in love and practice good manners. Jesus was always concerned about the well-being of others even in the way he chose to walk among them in perfect behavior.

Everyday Princess Manners

Keep your space clean and neat.

Say please and thank you.

Let others go before you.

Be on time.

Keep your hands clean.

Share.

Knock before entering.

Keep your opinions of others between you and God.

Show respect to your elders by referring to them as ma'am or sir.

Saying, "Excuse me please" is a nice way to say move.

Blow your nose in the bathroom when possible and wash hands afterward.

Do not pick your nose.

Push your chair in.

If you open it, close it back up.

If you turn it on, turn it off.

If you unlock it, take the time to lock it back.

If you break something that doesn't belong to you, be quick to admit you were at fault.

If you can't fix it, ask someone who is able to.

If you borrow it, return it in a reasonable amount of time.

If you value something, take care of it.

If you make a mess, don't expect someone to clean it up for you, clean it up yourself.

If you move it out of place, put it back where it goes.

If you don't know how to operate it, ask for help.

If it is not for you to know, then mind your own business.

If someone asks you a question, answer with a kind word and in a kind tone of voice.

If you are yelled at, don't yell back.

Don't repay evil for evil. Instead pray that person.

Don't walk by trash or an item on the floor; make an effort to pick it up and put it where it belongs.

♛ Princess Table Manners

A princess must learn the importance of elegant dining. Some dining skills are mechanical like holding eating utensils, drinking from the right glass, spitting out unwanted foods, and eating spaghetti without getting it all over your shirt. And some skills are social like who sits where, how to eat and talk at the same time, and how to deal with a bug or hair in your food. There are three dining styles; American, Continental, and Barbarian.

There are also many table settings and abbreviations of each. The most common table setting you will find a glass, plate, knife, spoon, fork, and napkin. For a more formal dinner setting, you may find three or four forks, two spoons, three knifes, the dinner plate, a bread plate, and as many as six glasses. You may find the napkin placed either beneath the forks, in the plate, in a glass, or at the left of the forks.

The most common dining question is what to do with all that silverware and which one do I use first. It is very simple when you understand the reason for placement. First, to the left you will find the forks and your dinner roll. Rule—left has four letters, fork has four letters, and roll has four letters. Second, to the right you will find the knives, spoons, and water glass. Rule—right has five letters, knife has five letters, and glass has five letters. The eating utensils are placed in the order of food to be served. Rule—start from the outside and work your way inside.

Bread—if passed in a basket, take one out and pass the basket to your right. Place your bread on your bread plate if one is available, if not place it on the top left of your dinner plate. Don't butter the entire roll at one time, instead tear in half and butter as you eat.

Soup—is usually brought out as a course of the meal. The soup spoon is on the far right side or is brought out with the soup bowl. Rule: spoon soup away from you, never slurp, or blow to cool. Instead, spoon soup from the top and sip from the side of the spoon and when finished leave spoon in bowl.

Salad—is brought out as a course of the meal or is already placed on the table. Your salad fork is on the left side of the dinner fork and is always the smaller of the two. If salad is served with the main course, there will be no salad fork. Cut large pieces of lettuce with a knife and never drench your salad with dressing.

Main Dinner Course—if it is meat, cut small pieces as you eat. Don't cut the entire steak at once. Instead of sawing to cut, gently stroke with your knife until a piece is cut off. Your dinner fork is the one closest to the dinner plate and is the largest fork on the table.

Desert—is usually brought out after the main course is served. You will find the desert fork and spoon placed horizontally on the desert plate or on the table above the dinner plate.

Coffee—is offered by placing a coffee cup upside down on a saucer and to the right of the dinner plate. If you would like to be served, simply turn coffee cup over.

Dining Tips

Avoid licking your fingers

It is rude to burp aloud

If you need to remove food from your mouth, remember these rules: in with a fork, out with a fork; in with fingers, out with fingers.

Do not talk with your mouth full. If you have to talk, cover mouth with your hand.

Squeeze lemon wedges with a spoon inside glass or squeeze over glass and shield with hand. Leave the lemon wedge in glass.

Don't make a scene when you see something in your food—remove it discreetly and without comment. You may ask waiter quietly for another serving.

When taking a drink, look down at your glass instead of looking around

Place your napkin in your lap and not around your neck

Place silverware in the 10/20 position when finished eating

When finished eating, place your napkin in your dish

Ask to be excused and leave napkin in chair

Use your silverware instead of your fingers

Sit up straight and tall

Taste foods before seasoning

Don't double dip

Don't hug your plate and keep elbows off the table

Thank the cook, waiter, or host

Eat over your plate

Twirl spaghetti on fork by using a spoon

Finger Foods

Potato chips	French Fries
French Fries	Chicken nuggets
Carrots	Pizza
Celery	Broccoli
Cauliflower	Bread
Crackers	Tacos

This is small list of foods you can eat with your fingers.

♛ Princess Phone Manners and E-Etiquette

Consider your tone and the loudness of your voice when talking

Be respectful in public places like meeting halls, school, church, restaurants, movie theaters, or in a store

Turn phone on silent or off when in a quiet place

Don't text and walk at the same time.

Keep your head up when walking and your phone in your pocket

Keep up with your phone and be responsible.

Don't use your phone in bed, make it your resting place

Give tech a rest. Turn off and Tune in to others

Avoid talking on the phone or texting when driving a car

Don't make prank calls

Say hello and identify yourself to a caller

Don't hang up on someone

Consider the time of day when calling

Only call 911 in an emergency

Check over emails for accuracy before sending

Avoid forwarding junk mail

Make email short and to the point

Use subject line for details

Reply promptly to incoming emails, or leave an auto reply until you have the time.

School Manners

Respect others—their property, feelings, and authority

Don't be loud and use an appropriate tone

Don't run in the building

Walk on the right side of the hallway

Follow school rules without complaining

Do more than what is expected of you

Don't interrupt an adult conversation

Always ask for permission

Raise your hand and don't blurt out loud

Show good sportsmanship

Help others when they need help

Use time wisely

Come to class prepared—bring all required material, have more than one sharp pencil on hand, and have assignments completed and ready to turn in

Be courteous to everyone

Don't be a bully and turn in someone who is

Don't be a tattle tail

Talk only when you have permission

Keep you space neat

Keep you chair pushed in

Don't stand over someone when they are in conversation with someone else; wait your turn

Respect school property

Don't slam doors

Gossiping and forming cliques are disrespectful

👑 Lunch Room Manners

Don't cram your mouth; chew then swallow

Don't gulp down your food with your drink

Save talk for after lunch

Don't share food or offer it to others

Don't comment on other people's meals or their eating styles

Leave table clean; pick-up trash even if it isn't yours

Stand in line quietly and don't push or shove

Report spills or messes to a teacher

Use fork or spoon to eat your food

👑 School Bus Manners

Don't scream and yell

Stay seated

Don't change from seat to seat

Don't leave trash

Don't talk to the bus driver when the bus is moving

Keep belongings in your seat or next to you

Follow rules

Watch for cars when loading and unloading

Keep your feet out of the seat and center aisle. Help watch out for others!

Thank You Notes

A thank you note is a great way to show appreciation. When sending a thank you note, make it personal by using your own handwriting. A thank you note should be sent within a week's time. Don't wait a month to send it. There are many reasons to send a thank you note. Send a thank you note when someone gives you a gift, does something nice for you, helps you complete a task or job, takes time out of their schedule to help, when you are invited to a party, or when you stay at a guest's home for more than two days. There are many ways you can show appreciation and say thank you. It says a lot about a person's character when they take the time to say thank you.

How to be Thoughtful of Others

Everyone deserves a nice gesture from time to time. A card, phone call, or a simple hello is a great way to help brighten someone's day. Think of others and treat them as you would like to be treated. For example, keep a list of birthdays, anniversaries, and special occasions handy. Prepare ahead of time cards or letters to send. Keep special occasion cards on hand like thinking of you, you're the greatest, thank you, you're special, and holiday cards. Christianity is about loving one another and giving to others.

Minding Your Manners

Is your behavior acceptable to others?	Always Sometimes Never
Do you use kind words like please and thank you?	Always Sometimes Never
Do you practice good table manners?	Always Sometimes Never
Do you keep your space nice and neat?	Always Sometimes Never
Are you respectful to those in authority?	Always Sometimes Never

How can you improve the way you treat others and yourself?

_____

_____

_____

What things can you do to improve your behavior?

_____

_____

_____

Do you think God is happy with the way you treat others?

Yes or No. Why?

_____

_____

_____

Princess Bible Verse

I Peter 3:3, 4

"Let not yours be the (merely) external adorning with (elaborate) interweaving and knotting of the hair, the wearing of jewelry, or changes of clothes; But let it be the inward adorning and beauty of the hidden person of the heart, with the incorruptible and unfading charm of a gentle and peaceful spirit, which (is not anxious or wrought up, but) is very precious in the sight of God."

♛ Princess Beauty Tips

Hair rollers come in many different styles and sizes. They are a great way for a princess to set curls in her hair. It takes time to set them, but in the end the curl was worth the effort. Minding your manners can be compared to setting rollers in your hair. Although it takes time and effort to behave correctly, it is always worth it in the end.

♛ Princess Confessions

I will use good manners and be nice to everyone, including my own family, even when I do not feel like it. I am a representation of Christ Jesus and my behavior should reflect him.

♛ Princess Prayer

Father, thank you for helping me to be on my best behavior every day. Teach me to use good manners, be quick to be courteous, and lovely to everyone. Help me resist the temptation to be rude to others. Thank you, Lord, for always loving me no matter how many mistakes I may make. I know it is your will for me to live unto righteousness and to always reflect your likeness in everything I do. In Jesus' name, Amen.

♛ Princess Challenge

Show kindness and gratitude by sending a thank you card to someone.

♛ Princess Crown Thought

But as the one who called you is holy, you yourselves also be holy in all your conduct and manner of living. I Peter 1:15

Princess Journaling Assignment

Make a list of good manners that you use every day, and then make a list of the bad ones. Establish a plan on how you can use good manners all the time.

Write Your Own Prayer:

Righteousness

Lisa Delmedico Harris

Chapter 17

God and Righteousness

The Bible has a lot to say about righteousness and how important it is to have in our everyday life. Righteousness is simply having Jesus in your heart and doing what is right. You are the righteousness of God in Christ Jesus. Jesus is the righteous one.

The American Heritage Dictionary describes righteousness as being morally upright, and without guilt or sin.[1] It also describes the righteous as a group of people. If you are doing what is right and living unto righteousness, you are part of a group of the unordinary. Most people don't do what is right; instead they compromise and blend in with the social norm. In whatever you do, pursue love and righteousness. Never allow the compromising thoughts of your mind hinder you from doing the right thing. Doing what is right will reward you with good character. Having good character is a trait of righteousness. God is righteous, and if he lives inside your heart you will live unto him and do what is right—this is considered righteousness. Work on building a character of good moral standing rather than one full of guilt and sin.

God created Adam and placed him in a beautiful garden. The Garden of Eden provided Adam with all the right and good things. The garden was a perfect place filled with beautiful things. There was no doubt it was heaven on earth. When God created Adam and placed him into the garden, he gave him the job of caring for the garden. But not only was Adam to tend to the garden, he was also to live unto righteousness. Live unto God, fellowship with him and dwell with him. Adam did what God asked of him and obeyed his commands, until one day he compromised. He and Eve chose to disobey God and broke fellowship with him by breaking the covenant of righteousness. They traded in rightness for a moment of pleasure. They indulged in self-gratification and suffered the consequences.

The Bible reads, for the wages of sin is death; but the gift of God is eternal life through Jesus Christ our Lord.[2] Just as if you were working a job and getting paid, so shall you be paid for your choices in life. However, when you live unto righteousness and work for God, your paycheck will be full of blessing. Jesus, the righteous one, has redeemed you from sin and all the unrighteousness brought about when Adam chose to compromise.

The Bible is full of scriptures on righteousness and gives us many examples of how we should live unto righteousness. God's ways are the right ways and man's ways are the wrong ways. God's ways are always perfect. Although you may have a conflict of interest with someone's ways of right or wrong, remember you are to be a leading example of righteousness, and you will win others by the way you choose not to compromise. Righteousness will always turn away evil and bring you peace, joy, and a clear conscious.

How do you become righteous? First, you accept the righteous one, Jesus Christ, into your heart and make him Lord over your life and then you will become the righteousness of God in Christ Jesus.[3] Secondly, do what is right. Making healthy decisions in everyday situations will cause righteousness. Thirdly, become skilled in the word of righteousness[4] or the word of God. You will never grow-up and become a fully matured Christian if you don't read the Bible and fellowship with righteousness. When you were a baby, your mother gave you a bottle with milk because you were not physically mature enough to take solid foods. But when you started to grow and mature physically, she started feeding you solid foods. The same is true for you spiritually. After you become saved and confess Jesus as your Lord, you should start "skilling" yourself in the word of righteousness by reading your Bible, going to church, and praying. Faith comes by hearing, and hearing by the word of God.[5] If you want to mature in righteousness, eat of God's word. The word is a food supply that will feed and nourish your body physically, mentally, and spiritually. It supplies the proper nutrients that will help you grow and become the matured adult or elder of Christianity that God intends you to become. He does not intend for you to stay a baby all your life. He wants you to grow and mature in his word, so you will grow spiritually and know right from wrong,[6] and be able to help others. Hide the Word of God in your heart so that you will know how to become righteous.[7]

Here are some ways you can live unto righteousness. The Bible says you can live unto righteousness by living by God's laws, keeping his commandments, doing it God's way and not your own, and by heeding the words of God. You can live unto righteousness by walking in the fruit of the spirit: love, patience, kindness, gentleness, self-control, joy, peace, long-suffering, goodness, and faithfulness, against such there is no law.[8] You can live unto righteousness by fixing your mind the Word of God and thinking what is right. Think on these things, whatever things are true, noble, pure, lovely, of a good report, anything of virtue, and praiseworthy, meditate on these things.[9] You can live unto righteousness by staying pure before God, obeying God and taking his words, his instructions, his laws, and his commandments to heart. You can live unto righteousness by staying in obedience to God, obeying God and taking his words, his instructions, his laws, and his commandments to heart. You can live unto righteousness by obeying your parents and other authorities over you (Ephesians 6:1).

There are many instructions in the Word of God about righteousness. I encourage you to study on the subject of righteousness and what God considers "being and doing right." Awake to righteousness and do not sin! (I Corinthians 15:34). There are not only things you can do to practice righteousness, but there are also benefits you will reap from it.

Being righteous will cause God to hear your prayers, Proverbs 15:29.

Being righteous will cause God to protect and safely guard you in all your ways, Proverbs 18:10.

Being righteous will cause you to shine and stand out, Matthew 13:43.

Being righteous will bring peace, and the effect of it, quietness and assurance forever, Isaiah 32:17.

Righteousness leads to life, Proverbs 11:19.

The righteous will flourish (prosper) like foliage, Proverbs 11:28.

Being righteous brings God's blessing and favor, Proverbs 10:6.

Being righteous means desires shall be granted, Proverbs 10:24.

If you know that he is righteous, you know that everyone who practices righteousness is born of him, 1 John 2:29.

God is Righteous, Jeremiah 33:17. He is the Lord our Righteousness.

God loves righteousness, Hebrews 1:9. He loves righteousness and hates lawlessness.

God judges with righteousness, Isaiah 11:4. God is always good and right.

God gives righteousness to us, Isaiah 45:13. He gave us Jesus the righteous one.

God wears righteousness, Isaiah 11:5. God wears it like a belt around his loins.

It is fitting for us to fulfill all righteousness, Matthew. 3:15.

God will cause righteousness to spring forth, Isaiah 61:11.

For he made him who knew no sin to be sin for us, that we might become the righteousness of God in him, 2 Corinthians 5:21.

Princess Bible Verse

Proverbs 11:18-19

"The wicked man earns deceitful wages, but he who sows righteousness (moral and spiritual rectitude in every area and relation) shall have a sure reward [permanent and satisfying]. He who is steadfast in righteousness (uprightness and right standing with God) attains to life, but he who pursues evil does it to his own death."

Princess Beauty Tips

A princess always takes time to study and read the Bible. She knows that the wisdom and instructions inside can bring her health and prosperity. Righteousness comes only from the righteous one—Jesus. Spend time with righteousness and it will help you do what is right.

Princess Confessions

I confess I am the righteousness of God in Christ Jesus. I have the blood of Jesus Christ running through my veins and do all things by his strength.

Princess Prayer

Thank you, Father, for Jesus that through him I have been given everything that pertains to life and godliness. Father, I recognize that I need righteousness in my life. I pray that you will take my heart and mold it, take my mind and transform it through the power of your word, and take my life and conform it to be more like you--the righteous holy one. In Jesus' name, Amen.

Princess Challenge

Live more like Jesus every day. Make a decision to walk as he walked: in love and in peace.

Princess Crown Thought

God has made you worthy of his righteousness through the works of Jesus Christ.

Princess Journaling Assignment

Are you walking, talking, and acting as Jesus did? Do others see Him when they look at you? Make a list of the things you are doing to live unto righteousness.

Write Your Own Prayer:

Chapter 18

God and Your Relationships

God wants you to have good relationships with good people that will leave lasting impressions on your life. God uses people to sharpen you and challenge you to become a better person. A good relationship should encourage, strengthen, and uplift you. A good relationship will encourage you to walk closer with God. It is important to acknowledge God in the area of your relationships. Sometimes we take relationships for granted, and once they have ended, we realize how important they were to us. For example, some take their relationship with their parents for granted and treat them disrespectfully. People don't live forever, and we should treasure each day and every moment. Some people take their relationship with God for granted only acknowledging him whenever it is convenient or whenever they are in a crisis. God wants you to have a strong relationship with him and learn to trust him in everyday situations. He wants to be your best friend, and best friends stick with you through the good, the bad, and the ugly.

Relationships are like links in a chain. We need people in our life to be successful. God uses people and relationships to get us where we need to be in life. If you are willing to do God's will and submit to his ways, then you are setting yourself up for divine connections.

Most all of us will have many relationships—relationships with our parents, brothers, sisters, pastors, teachers, and grandparents. These relationships will all be important links in your chain of destiny and purpose. But your relationship with God will be your most important connection through relationship. Without Jesus as your best friend, your life will be out of balance. No other relationship without him will work. Jesus is the friend who will stick closer to you than a brother.[1] He will never let you down or give up on you. Jesus laid down his life for you just as a true friend would. He is always thinking of you and looking out for your best interest. Jesus gave his life for you because he wanted to more than a friend, he wanted to be your Savior. When he died on the cross for your sins, he had no guarantee that you would accept him as a friend. He did it in hopes that you would accept him. The Bible says, "Blessed are those who have not seen and yet have believed."[2] You are blessed because you call Jesus your friend.

God is good, and he loves you so much. He desires to have a relationship with you. He desires your friendship and your companionship. He desires you to spend time with him, talking, reading his word, and fellowshipping with him each day. God desires your company. You have been made in the likeness of God, and because of it, you will desire companionship with people. There is nothing wrong with having many relationships, but there is something wrong when you put them above your relationship with God. God is a jealous God.[3] Anything or anyone you put above God is considered an idol.

There is more to God than religion. Religion is man's ideas of God's expectations and has nothing to do with the real meaning of serving God. You should look into his word to find out his ideas and his ways. Don't rely on man's ideas. You can set in a church every Sunday morning, but it won't make you a Christian. You can set in a garage, but it won't make you a car. Maybe you go to church, love God, and read your Bible every day, but can you say you have a personal relationship with him? There is more to Christianity than being a Christian. Christianity is a one-on-one experience—a relationship with a real person who loves and cares for you. Just like any relationship, you have to invest time and effort in getting to know one another. You can't expect to develop a close relationship with someone if you don't spend time with them as often as you can.

Best friends go everywhere together, they share everything, and they know one another, that is the way your relationship with God should be. He already knows everything about you, why not talk to him about your life and make him your best friend? Do you have a relationship with Jesus? Do you talk with him on a daily basis, fellowship with him as often as you can? Do you spend time reading his word and learning his ways? Do you recognize his voice as if it were your own father? Do you love him with all your mind, soul, body, and strength? The Bible says that tradition makes the word of God of no effect.[4] Your belief system if not based on the word of God, can hinder you from receiving all God has promised. People make traditions and beliefs from their own point of view rather than from the point of view of what God says. You should not let your religion or your own traditions hold you back. There is more to God than what you can think or imagine. God is a big God. Don't limit yourself by letting your religious traditions get in the way of his word. Don't be deceived in your own thinking and reasoning. Religion will keep you in your own thoughts and patterns of action. If you break away from a "religious spirit" and let go of the limitations you have of God then you will discover there were no limits at all. Jesus has given you freedom in this life. The freedom to serve him and enjoy the life he has given you. How can you truly enjoy everything in your life and be complete in Christ until you break free from the bondage of tradition and limitations? Don't let your traditions and ways of thinking keep you from going higher in your relationship with God.

Friendship

Are you looking for a friend? Someone you can bond with, share your time with, and talk to? A friend who is thoughtful, honest, kind and who will always love you for who you are? Do friendships like that really exist? You won't find these kinds of friendships on your own; you will need some divine help. Friendships may come and go, but lasting friendships can only come from God. If you are searching for a friend you can trust in and depend on, then stop looking and start praying. Ask God to send the friends he has already ordained for you, into your path. God loves you so much that he has even taken the time to make special friendships for you. There is someone waiting in the wings to meet you. Who knows where or how it will happen, but you can guarantee it will. The Bible says we have not because we ask not.[5] So if you want a good friend, a friend who will help, encourage, and strengthen you, then simply ask for one!

Having friendships that are God ordained are powerful tools for you to use on this earth. He establishes friendships for a purpose. It's called the power of agreement. Most of the time you are attracted to people with whom you agree and get along. The friends you choose to be in agreement with will play an important role in your future.

If you are in a relationship with someone who is not encouraging and edifying you, someone who is always keeping you in turmoil, pressuring you to compromise, and to *fit-in* with the social norm, then it is time to re-evaluate that relationship. Sometimes you may need to break off a relationship with a person in order to keep on the right path of righteousness. Compromising is not a part of being righteous. Examine the friends you have around you and the ones that influence you the most. Ask yourself this question: Are the friends in my life helping me to become a better person? Are they helping propel me into the future? Are they bringing strength to my life? If you can answer no to any of these questions then you need to take your friendships to God in prayer. Only through prayer will you find the right friends. Be honest with God. He knows your heart before you even ask. Ask him to remove counterfeit relationships and establish only those relationships which have been divinely planned for your life. Start asking God for divine relationships, divine set-ups, and divine assignments on a regular basis.

You don't have to be best friends with everyone; the key is to be friendly to everyone. But be cautious with whom you become close friends. There are many wolves dressed in sheep clothing, waiting to be used by the devil to help kill, steal, or destroy you and your future. It may not be easy to walk away from any relationship. But you have the power within you to overcome any disappointment and walk away with peace in your heart knowing you made the right decision. An ungodly friendship can be a distraction in your faith walk. Either a friendship can help your faith walk or it can hinder your faith walk. The Bible speaks of relationships in this way:

"Do not be unevenly yoked with unbelievers [do not make mismated alliances with them or come under a different yoke with them, inconsistent with your faith]. For what partnership have right living and right standing with God with iniquity and lawlessness? Or how can light have fellowship with darkness?"

II Corinthians 6:14

Therefore, since these [great] promises are ours, beloved, let us cleanse ourselves from everything that contaminates and defiles body and spirit, and bring [our] consecration to completeness in the [reverential] fear of God.

II Corinthians 7:1

The friends in your life are very important to your well-being, and God is very much concerned that you establish the right friendships in your life. Having the right friends in your life can help put you on the right path, and having the wrong ones in your life can put you on the wrong path. Only you can examine your friendships and determine if they are right for you. Don't be afraid to let go of a friendship if you know it is not right to continue, it could save your life in the end.

Sometimes God establishes certain relationships and friendships in our lives to only last for a season. There is a season and a time for everything, and that includes friendships. In one season of your life, you may need a friend that will lend a shoulder to cry on or an ear to listen. God is the only one who knows everything about you. He hears your every need, concern, and cry. God is your friend he is always there for you, and he will send someone your way to help you. In another season, you may need a special relationship with a person who can provide strength and wisdom. Good friends will help encourage and teach you to become a better person. They will help encourage you into a deeper relationship with God. Each friendship that is established in your life will play an important role. So don't worry about a friendship or relationship that has withered away. Don't beat yourself up over whether or not it was your fault, or wonder what went wrong in the friendship that caused it to end. Most of all, don't go chasing after those old friendships because you feel obligated or pressured. Instead, thank God for the opportunity you had to share in their life while the season lasted.

There is nothing like a divine relationship and friendship that has been established by God. Having a friendship that God has sought out for you instead of one that you have sought out for yourself is the best way to assure an excellent and well-planned friendship. As we grow older in life and our maturity level develops and expands, we learn that having the right friends around us only adds beauty to our lives. There is nothing like having a friend that you can count on and depend on, someone with whom you can connect and share. But even more so, having a special friend who will stand and agree with you in prayer. The power of agreement is a powerful tool, and a friend who will agree in prayer with you is a special friend. That is why we should be spiritually connected with the right people.

"Again I tell you, if two of you on earth agree (harmonize together, make a symphony together) about whatever [anything and everything] you may ask, it will come to pass and be done for them by my Father in heaven."

Matthew 18:19

A friend you can call a prayer partner is one of the keys to having victory in your life. The power of the tongue holds life or death. So remember to agree and talk about the positive and goods things of life with your friends. Not only speak good words so you can reap a good harvest, but speak good words about others so they can reap good benefits as well.

Notice in the above scripture says if two or more agree than it shall be done for them. Agreeing is the key. When you pray and use your faith things happen in the spirit realm that we cannot image. The Bible also states that when we as an individual pray, one thousand demonic powers go to flight, and when we pray as two or more ten thousand go to flight, *wow*! That is great news for believers and bad news for the powers of darkness. That is called the power of agreement. So the next time you are facing a situation that seems challenging and you need a little extra help getting through it, don't forget your power tool. Call your prayer partner friend, plug-in, and use the tool that will get you results.

Everything that is established in a friendship matters. Each aspect of that individual can be used to sharpen you. The princess Bible verse at the beginning of this chapter says, "Iron sharpens iron; so a man sharpens the countenance of his friend." We all need to be sharpened in different areas of our life. You may be weak in some areas that your friend may be strong in and vice versa. You both rub your abilities together to sharpen one another. This is how a good friendship should be. You should be sharpening your friend and your friend should be sharpening you. Don't remain dull and lifeless by choosing your own friends, but allow God to bring those friends into your life who will help you stay sharp at all times. Pray for your friends and their well-being. You don't have to be a part of the in-crowd to be popular. You are already popular in God's eyes just by being who you are. If you love God's word, keep his commandments, and always do what is right no matter what the situation, it will cause you to gain the respect of others and people will want to be your friend.

The Friendship Test

Ask yourself these questions about your current friendships.

Does my friend encourage and strengthen me?

___

Does my friend always find fault in me?

___

Does my friend control our friendship by always making the plans and dictating what we do?

___

Does my friend get jealous easily, especially when I am with others or when good things happen to me?

___

Does my friend keep me from being the person I really want to be?

___

Does my friendship include conversations about Jesus and His word?

___

Does my friend gossip and belittle others?

Does my friend help me when I need help?

Would my friend die for my sake? (Jesus died for us and we are called friends of God.)

Does my friend love me as she loves herself?

Does my friend stick with me in good and bad times?

Does my friend encourage me to read my Bible, pray more, and become closer to God?

Does my friend take from me and never give anything in return?

Does my friend edify and lift my spirits when I need to be lifted?

_____

_____

Does my friend encourage me to compromise?

_____

_____

Does my friend pressure me into things I do not want to do?

_____

_____

Does my friend sharpen me, challenge me, convict me, and encourage me to become better?

_____

_____

Make a list of the strengths and weaknesses in your friendship.

_____

_____

What do you expect in a friend?

_____

_____

Do my friends meet this expectation?

_____

_____

Dating

"Do not be unevenly yoked with unbelievers [do not make mismated alliances with them or come under a different yoke with them, inconsistent with your faith]. For what partnership have right living and right standing with God with iniquity and lawlessness? Or how can light have fellowship with darkness?"

2 Corinthians 6:14

The same principles to finding a friend can also be used in finding the right date and the right mate. God is interested in everything you do. He cares about the people you are friends with, the people you date, and the person you will one day marry. These people can play an important role in the outcome of your life. If you are looking forward to dating and you don't know how to go about it, then let's discuss some very important issues that need to be taken into consideration before you make the decision to go out on the first date or even say "I do."

God is interested in you and loves you so much. He has set aside people for you to date. God has also set aside that one man who is anointed to become your husband. Don't settle for second best—only settle for the *best*! Don't think for a moment you are not worthy of the best, because you are. You are God's child and God's children are royalty. Therefore, you are expected to have the best.

Always acknowledge God in all your ways and the Bible says he will guide and direct your paths, Proverbs 3:5-6. Before going out on that first date or walking down the aisle, make the decision to acknowledge the Lord first. Ask him to give you peace about your decision. Make sure you are being led by his spirit and not by your flesh.

By practice, the first thing we recognize about people is the way they look. We as a society hardly look beyond it. But we know that for many, beauty is only skin-deep. What we miss by being drawn to someone's appearance is their true intellect, their morality, and their values. The packaging may look good on the outside but what is on the inside will matter the most.

When finding someone to date, consider more than their looks consider the total package. Dating should always be handled with care. Handled carelessly could lead to destruction and even to complete devastation. The enemy has nothing but devastation, humiliation, shame, guilt, and the loss of your innocence planned for your life.

To avoid making wrong decisions, always stay true to you, *never* compromise and waver from the Word of God, and always do what it says about staying pure and holy in the sight of the Lord. In your life, ask the Lord to remove all counterfeits from your path, and to bring only those he has ordained for you to cross your path. Be in tune with God and his word instead of being in tune with your raging hormones. God made Eve to compliment Adam. God didn't make her to be inferior or second best.

Your male relationship should be one that compliments you and not one that is jealous or controlling of you. Never let another person become dominate over you. Instead, they should be uplifting you, encouraging you, and inspiring you to be the best you can be. Never allow anyone to shape and mold you into what they want you to be or even become. Stay true to who you are and don't change for anyone but God. You have the right to be yourself. You have the right to express yourself and your feelings. You have the right to say *no*, and most of all you have the right to make the decisions that will lead you to life or to death.

If you are looking to man to fulfill your every need, you will not find one. God is the only one who can completely fulfill you. Your life will never fit together perfectly until you have God in your life and let him rule and reign over you. You cannot be loved unless you first know God loves you. You cannot show love for someone else until you first learn to love yourself. You cannot be happy until you first learn to rejoice in the Lord always and let his happiness fill your heart. Man will fail you every time, but God Almighty will never fail you.

Stop looking and start praying for the people God has ordained to come to you. Don't search when God has already done the searching for you. Why double the work of righteousness when your work has already been done? God has a plan and you are part of it. You have not been over-looked. Let the relationships come to you rather than you going after them. However, you can sit in your room in fear or wait for things to knock on your door. Open the door of opportunity by making connections with others by being friendly and getting involved in the lives of others.

Important Qualities in a Date

They have love and compassion for others—perfect love comes from above.

Their faith/belief system should be in harmony with yours—do not be unevenly yoked together.

They put God first in their life, then others, then themselves.

They are thoughtful, sincere, considerate, and respectful of you and of others.

They have goals, dreams, desires, and they are not afraid to work.

They are respectful of your body and of your values.

They are not jealous, domineering, or controlling of you.

They keep God's ways, his commandments, and love his word.

They are spirit led and never make decisions without praying first.

They care about your hopes, your dreams, and support your future.

They celebrate you and care about all that concerns you.

If someone truly loves you they will not only say they love you, they will show it.

These may seem like many qualities, but they are essential in having a healthy relationship. God cares about who you connect with in your life. Just as a friend can be an important tool in life, your mate can be as well. It is important to agree with one another. Although there will be times of disagreements and disappointments, make sure your relationship is built on a firm foundation so that nothing can shake it. Base your relationships on integrity and character instead of on appearance. You will have plenty of time to date and plenty of time to be married. Don't rush either of them. Both can be a wonderful experience if they are started in the right way.

♛ Things to Remember When Dating

Never compromise your values.

Never let a boy touch you in an inappropriate place.

Never say "Yes" when you really mean "No."

Remember your body is the temple of the Holy Spirit.

Kissing, cuddling, and caressing are meant for marriage.

There are many fish in the sea, do not settle for the first one that jumps out.

Ask God to do the fishing for you.

Let the boy pursue you, instead of you pursuing the boy.

Don't be deceived by looks, only admire the heart.

Let time have its way and everything will fall in time with it.

♛ Princess Bible Verse

Proverbs 27:17

"As iron sharpens iron, so a man sharpens the countenance of his friend."

👑 Princess Beauty Tips

A princess never kisses on the first date and is committed to keeping her purity. However, it is okay to hold hands on the first date. Your relationships are a lot like holding hands. They should fit together perfectly and never pull you down. Allow God to hold your hand and walk you through every relationship.

👑 Princess Confessions

I confess I will choose friends wisely and with the wisdom of God. I will acknowledge his ways in all that I do. I expect divine relationships, divine set-ups, and divine assignments every day of my life.

👑 Princess Prayer

Father, I pray for divine friendships, only those friendships and relationships you have ordained and prearranged for me before the foundations of the earth. I ask your help to resist the temptation to want to fit-in. I choose to be set apart from unbelievers and be yoked together with believers. I know it is your will for my life to have good friends. I pray for good friends to find me, love me, sharpen me, and strengthen me. Thank you for the relationships and divine connections. Lord, I pray for the strength to resist the temptations of the flesh. I need your strength to help me stay pure and holy in your sight. I pray for the husband you have planned for me to marry may he remain true to you, pure, and holy. In Jesus' name, Amen.

👑 Princess Challenge

Instead of choosing friends by popular vote, cast your cares on the Lord and allow him to bring good friends to you.

👑 Princess Crown Thought

Love isn't just a feeling, it is a set of behaviors, actions, and choices.

Princess Journaling Assignment

Are you spending time with the right friends? Or are you trying to fit in and be accepted by those who don't really care about you? Write down the names of your friends and how they sharpen your life. What is your ideal friend?

_____

_____

_____

_____

_____

_____

_____

_____

_____

_____

_____

_____

_____

_____

_____

_____

_____

_____

Write Your Own Prayer:

Chapter 19

God and Your Future

Have you ever had a dream, maybe a dream of becoming a doctor, movie star, or even a model? The fact is, we are all full of dreams and desires—it is what helps keep us motivated in life. Dreams are hopes for the future. A desire is a passion to fulfill that dream. A passion is a strong connection to the dream.

What do you love to do? What you love to do with all your heart is tied to your passion. God has given everyone dreams and desires. You have had dreams and desires planted into your heart from the very beginning of time. You have been given a divine dream seed and without this dream, you will never walk in the perfect plan for your life. God has a vision for you. He has a dream for you. He wants you to pursue and go after your dreams. Without a dream you have no vision. Without a vision in life, the word of God says that people will perish, see Proverbs 29:18. People die prematurely because there is no hope or vision in their life. Hope deferred makes the heart sick, but when the desire comes, it is a tree of life, see Proverbs 13:12.

God has predestined your life before the earth was even established in the heavens. He knew in order to accomplish his plan it would take dreams and desires. You make choices each day to either pursue your dreams or to sit back and let them pass you by. *Pursuing your dreams will help you in finding and fulfilling your destiny. You have a calling and a purpose in this life. Dreams and desires will help you arrive at your destination point. You may have a dream in your heart of one day becoming a teacher, a lawyer, or a mother of three children; whatever the dream, it all is important in the plan of God. God wants you to fulfill your destiny. It is his plan for you to prosper[1] and live a happy fulfilled life. God gets excited when he sees you working to accomplish your dreams and desires. He is more excited about you fulfilling your destiny than you are. By fulfilling his destiny for your life, you are working for his kingdom.

God doesn't give you a dream and not furnish you with the tools you need to accomplish it. He has equipped you for every good work. He has given you gifts and talents to work with. These are tools needed to make your dreams come true. Make a point of asking the Lord to make known to you your gifts and talents. The Word of God says, ask and you shall receive. Talents and gifts are things you are good at doing. If you are unsure of your gifts and talents, write down all the things you are good at doing and all the things you are not good at doing. This will help you determine your strengths and weaknesses; with this information, you can capitalize on your strengths and improve on your weaknesses. There is nothing inside you that cannot be used by God, including your weaknesses.

With each dream, you must have a plan or a goal to achieve that dream. Goals are a part of the vision. They help you and encourage you to press toward the dream. Without a plan, you won't get very far. Planning and working go hand and hand. You cannot accomplish a plan unless you work at getting it done. Work is the key ingredient in the recipe for success. You cannot prosper or fulfill your calling by sitting around wishing. Wishing and hoping do not operate together. A wish is simply a shallow wishful thought, but hoping is connected to faith in your heart. It is a sense of knowing and believing it will happen. Never confess, "I am wishing and hoping," instead say, "I am praying and I believe I receive by faith."

A dream or desire sparks passion, passion sparks hope, and hope sparks faith. Without believing you have received that which you have prayed for, you will not see your dream come true. If you do not believe or have hope and faith, you will not accomplish your dreams. Faith will determine your destiny. If you want to stroll down "Destiny Lane," you have to walk by faith and use your gifts and talents to get you there. Just believe in yourself and in God to help you get where you need to be. You have to step out into a dream and walk in it. The only way you can learn how to swim is if you get into the water. Don't second guess yourself. You can do all things through Christ Jesus who gives you strength.[2] Don't second guess the dreams God has given you and wonder if they will ever come to pass, know that they will and declare, it shall happen. But remember this: not every dream will work out the way you think it should, but each step you take to pursue those dreams will bring your closer to the perfect will of God.

People can dream dreams, but only big dreams come from God. When you know you can't achieve it on your own abilities, then you know it is a God-given dream. You have probably been told by someone you can do anything you set your heart to do. But this statement is not true. You can only do those things which God has ordained for you to do. It is your responsibility to seek the perfect will of God for your life. Everyone is called to do a special work for the kingdom of God. But without being in the perfect will and pursing God's dreams and desires, you will not fulfill the call. When you follow your own selfish ambitions you will never enter into a place of rest, happiness, or contentment.

God has the perfect plan, the perfect dream, the perfect place, and the perfect time for your dream to come true. Set your goals, write down a vision list, make plans, work toward your dreams, and never give up. You are destined for greatness!

Princess Purpose

Answer these simple questions to determine more about your princess purpose.

What are you passionate about?

_____

_____

What do you enjoy doing?

_____

_____

What are your strengths and weaknesses?

_____

_____

What comes natural to you or is easy?

What are you interested in doing as a career?

What do you like to do that makes you happy?

Describe your personality.

What do you spend the majority of your time thinking about?

What makes you angry the most is what you are called to change or perfect. What makes you angry?

What do you what to do for the kingdom of God? Do you know your calling?

Vision List

And the Lord answered me and said, Write the vision and engrave it so plainly upon tablets that everyone who passes may [be able to] read [it easily and quickly] as he hastens by. For the vision is yet for an appointed time and it hastens to the end [fulfillment]; it will not deceive or disappoint. Though it tarry, wait [earnestly] for it, because it will surely come; it will not be behindhand on its appointed day.

Habakkuk 2:2-3

"Where there is no vision (no redemptive revelation of God), The people perish; But he who keeps the law (of God, which includes that of man) blessed (happy, fortunate, and enviable) is he.

Proverbs 29:18

Keep a notebook of your vision. Make a list and name it "Vision List." Write everything you have a passion to do in life. For example, everything you want to do, everyone you want to meet, every place you would like to go. Also, write down your dreams and desires. Keep this list in front of you as a reminder. Pray over your list and see them take shape in your life and come to pass. Check your vision daily and make changes and additions as necessary.

Goals

Set goals so that you can accomplish them. Each day write a list of things you want to accomplish by the end of that day. Keep a list of short and long-term goals. Strive to achieve and complete your lists each day. Goals will bring you closer to your perfect place in God's kingdom. For example, set daily goals, weekly goals, bi-weekly goals, monthly goals and even yearly goals. You are most likely to accomplish them if you write them down and keep them in front of you.

Anticipating Your Future

Dream a dream.

Write your vision down, Habakkuk 2:2.

Study to show yourself approved.

Manage your finances to save for your dream.

Invest time in yourself by:

Staying physically fit.

Eating healthy foods.

Continually renewing your mind with the Word of God daily.

Stay strong in your body, soul, and spirit.

Don't give up and don't lose heart, for in due season it will come to pass.

Set goals short-term and long-term.

Pray without ceasing, mostly in the spirit.

Delight yourself in the Lord.

Confess your dreams into reality by speaking and believing.

Water your dreams by giving thanks to the Lord and reminding him of his promises.

Set your mind on things above, forget the past, and run toward the future.

Princess Bible Verse

Psalm 37:4

"Delight yourself also in the Lord, and he will give you the desires and secret petitions of your heart."

Princess Beauty Tips

A mirror is also referred to as a looking glass. It is a piece of material that gives a reflection of an image. When a princess looks into a mirror it reminds her of what she looks like. A mirror is much like a dream or vision. Just as a mirror shows a reflection of who we are, a dream shows us who we can become. Keep the vision of your dream in front of you.

Princess Confessions

I will have the desires of my heart because I choose to delight myself in the Lord. I know God is working on my behalf, and he never sleeps and never slumbers. I will fulfill the calling on my life.

Princess Prayer

Father, it is a blessing just to know you are my Heavenly Father and that you love me. I am so grateful to be called the daughter of God. I trust my life in your hands, and I know we are working together for good. I pray the blessing of Abraham seek me to overtake me, so that I may walk, live, and be blessed beyond measure. I pray you will continue to place my feet in the places that will lead me into my prearranged destiny. I also pray you will continue to set up relationships, divine appointments, and divine connections, which will result in divine manifestations. Help me to be quick to obey and hear your voice. Teach me your voice, so I will be quick to go and do those things for you, which you have purposed in your heart for me to do. In Jesus' name, Amen.

Princess Challenge

Set your sights higher. Ask bigger and start preparing now!

Princess Crown Thought

Give flight to your dreams by believing they can come to pass.

Princess Journaling Assignment

Set goals for your life. Start by writing down your vision and dreams and referring to them often. Make some short-term and long-term goals to accomplish your dream. Make a note as to where you want to be in one year, in three years, and even ten years.

Princess Journaling Assignment

Set goals for your life. Start by writing down your vision and dreams and referring to them often. Make some short-term and long-term goals to accomplish your dream. Make a note as to where you want to be in one year, in three years, and even ten years.

_____

_____

_____

_____

_____

_____

_____

_____

_____

_____

_____

_____

_____

People I would like to meet:

_____

_____

Things I would like to have:

_____

_____

Places I would like to go:

_____

_____

Things I would like to do:

_____

_____

My goal for today is:

_____

_____

My goal for the week:

_____

_____

My goal for one year:

_____

_____

My goal for three years:

_____

_____

My goal for ten years:

_____

_____

Chapter 20

God and Your Health

Your health depends a lot on the way you take care of your body. If you neglect your body and do not care for it properly, you could become unhealthy. For example, if you continue to eat a lot of sugar, you could end up with diabetes. If you continue to smoke or drink alcohol in excess, you could end up with cancer or liver disease. The choices you make play an important part in your health. God has given us wisdom in his word to teach us how to stay healthy physically and spiritually. But he has also given doctors wisdom to help people as well. Being healthy and walking in healing solely depends on your dedication to the word and the choice of taking care of your body to the best of your ability. You have been given authority over the devil, sickness, and disease. Don't let him steal your health and destroy your body. God needs you to be healthy in order to be a witness for him. Sickness and disease is not a part of God's perfect will for your life.

Healing is for everyone. Although some would disagree, Jesus did pay the price for our healing when he bore himself on the tree and took the stripes upon his back. Health and healing was paid for at the cross. People were never meant to carry the burden of sickness or disease. God does not place sickness and disease on people to teach them a lesson or to change the lives of others. How would dying of cancer or from a calamity bring joy into someone's life and teach a lesson? Jesus went about healing the sick and delivering them from their infirmities and he has given us a personal angel to keep and preserve us in all our ways. God does not have ownership of sickness or disease. God intends you to live happy, healthy, and prosperous. He has come to give us life in abundance, not take it away. The curse of sickness and disease was placed on the earth when Adam forfeited his authority over to the devil in the Garden of Eden. When Adam and Eve sinned in the garden, their sin brought about the curse on the earth. In Deuteronomy 28, God lists the blessings and curses that can come upon a person if they heed or do not heed the voice of the Lord God and observe carefully all his commandments.

"Christ purchased our freedom [redeeming us] from the curse (doom) of the Law [and its condemnation] by [Himself] becoming a curse for us, for it is written [in the Scriptures], Cursed is everyone who hangs on a tree (is crucified)."

Galatians 3:13

You have been redeemed from the curse through the redemption blood of Jesus Christ. His blood has freed you from the yoke of bondage of sickness and disease. Recognize your authority in Christ Jesus and stand up against bodily affliction. You have been given the blood of Jesus, the name of Jesus, and the word of Jesus (the Bible) as weapons to break the bondage of sickness and disease on your life and even the lives of others. Speak the word of God and plead the blood of Jesus over yourself and your family and believe in your heart that it is working in your behalf.

Everyone has this image of God as someone who sits on a throne and plays bingo all day with the lives of people. Our life is not a number in the bingo basket waiting to be called. Although our life is ordained by God, the choices we make determine blessing and cursing. We have been given the power of life or death. Jesus tells us in John 10:10 that, "The thief comes only in order to steal and kill and destroy. I came that they may have and enjoy life, and have it in abundance (to the full, till it overflows)." We have life in abundance through Jesus Christ. Being afflicted does not produce abundance. Abundance is overflow and affliction takes away and depletes a body of its abundance. The devil has spread vicious lies about sickness and disease. He has caused people to believe that sickness and disease is a part of life, and that we should just accept it. The devil has also caused us to believe that God is responsible for the bad that comes on us. Let me get one thing straight—God does not make you suffer through affliction to make you a better person! The devil is the only one who takes advantage of you through pain and bodily affliction. The devil is a liar! God is a good God and he only brings blessing and goodness into your life.

"For the wages of which sin pays is death, but the [bountiful] free gift of God is eternal life through (in union with) Jesus Christ our Lord."

Romans 6:23

If you are sick in body and in need of healing, read the word of God and pray for his wisdom. Faith cometh by hearing and hearing by the Word of God.[1] Healing comes by faith and doing what God instructs you to do to be healthy. Hearing the word of God and believing in your heart will stretch your faith muscle. Don't ever say you don't have faith; you do have faith, but it is up to you to determine the amount you use. We have all been given the same measure of faith. Know what God's will is for your life by reading and studying his word. You don't know someone's will unless they first tell you. God's will for you is to prosper and to be in good health[2] all the time. Confess God's promises over your life every day. Read and speak aloud healing scriptures and take it like medicine—three times a day. Use your authority and command sickness and disease to leave your body and your family. Healing is not something you have to pray for or work at achieving, it is already yours; it is a benefit of salvation.

Healing Scriptures

"Christ purchased our freedom [redeeming us] from the curse (doom) of the Law [and its condemnation] by [himself] becoming a curse for us, for it is written [in the Scriptures], Cursed is everyone who hangs on a tree (is crucified)."

Galatians 3:13

"Surely he has borne our griefs (sicknesses, weaknesses, and distresses) and carried our sorrows and pains [of punishment], yet we [ignorantly] considered him stricken, smitten, and afflicted by God [as if with leprosy]. But he was wounded for our transgressions, he was bruised for our guilt and iniquities; the chastisement [needful to obtain] peace and well-being for us was upon him, and with the stripes [that wounded] him we are healed and made whole."

Isaiah 53:4, 5

"Confess to one another therefore your faults (your slips, your false steps, your offenses, your sins) and pray [also] for one another, that you may be healed and restored [to a spiritual tone of mind and heart]. The earnest (heartfelt, continued) prayer of a righteous man makes tremendous power available [dynamic in its working]."

James 5:16

"He personally bore our sins in his [own body] on the tree [as on an altar and offered himself on it], that we might die (cease to exist) to sin and live to righteousness. By his wounds you have been healed."

I Peter 2:24

"Beloved, I pray that you may prosper in every way and [that your body] may keep well, even as [I know] our soul keeps well and prospers."

III John 2

"But no weapon that is formed against you shall prosper, and every tongue that shall rise against you in judgment you shall show to be in the wrong. This [peace, righteousness, security, triumph over opposition] is the heritage of the servants of the Lord [those in whom the ideal Servant of the Lord is reproduced]; this is the righteousness or the vindication which they obtain from me [this is that which I impart to them as their justification], says the Lord."

Isaiah 54:17

"Bless (affectionately, gratefully praise) the Lord, O my soul, and forget not [one of] all his benefits, who forgives [every one of] all your iniquities, who heals [each one of] all your diseases, who redeems your life from the pit and corruption, who beautifies, dignifies, and crowns you with loving-kindness and tender mercy; who satisfies your mouth [your necessity and desire at your personal age and situation] with good so that your youth, renewed, is like the eagle's [strong, overcoming, soaring]!"

Psalms 103:2-5

"You shall serve the Lord your God; he shall bless your bread and water, and I will take sickness from your midst."

Exodus 23:25

"He sends forth his word and heals them and rescues them from the pit and destruction."

Psalm 107:20

"My son, attend to my words; consent and submit to my sayings. Let them not depart from your sight; keep them in the center of your heart. For they are life to those who find them, healing and health to all their flesh."

Proverbs 4:20-22

Authority in Christ

"Which he exerted in Christ when he raised him from the dead and seated him at his [own] right hand in the heavenly [places], Far above all rule and authority and power and dominion and every name that is named [above every title that can be conferred], not only in this age and in this world, but also in the age and the world which are to come."

Ephesians 1:20-21

"You shall tread upon the lion and adder; the young lion and the serpent shall you trample underfoot."

Psalm 91:13

"Truly I tell you, whatever you forbid and declare to be improper and unlawful on earth must be what is already forbidden in heaven, and whatever you permit and declare proper and lawful on earth must be what is already permitted in heaven. Again I tell you, if two of you on earth agree (harmonize together, make a symphony together) about whatever [anything and everything] they may ask, it will come to pass and be done for them by my Father in heaven".

Matthew 18:18-19

"For You have put everything in subjection under his feet. Now in putting everything in subjection to man, he left nothing outside [of man's] control. But at present we do not yet see all things subjected to him [man]."

Hebrews 2:8

"For he [the Father] has put all things in subjection under his [Christ's] feet. But when it says, All things are put in subjection [under him], it is evident that he [himself] is excepted who does the subjecting of all things to him."

I Corinthians 15:27

"Jesus approached and, breaking the silence, said to them, all authority (all power of rule) in heaven and on earth has been given to me."

Matthew 28:18

"And God blessed them and said to them, Be fruitful, multiply, and fill the earth, and subdue it [using all its vast resources in the service of God and man]; and have dominion over the fish of the sea, the birds of the air, and over every living creature that moves upon the earth."

Genesis 1:28

"Behold! I have given you authority and power to trample upon serpents and scorpions, and [physical and mental strength and ability] over all the power that the enemy [possesses]; and nothing shall in any way harm you."

Luke 10:19

Tips on Staying Healthy

Cough in the curve of your arm instead of the palm of your hand.

Sneeze in a tissue, or in your arm if one is not available quick enough.

Wash your hands often, especially after you have touched your nose or used the restroom.

Read God's word.

Quote healing scriptures and confess them over yourself daily.

Confess you are the healed of the Lord each day.

Use your spiritual authority and stand firm against the wiles of the devil, especially sickness and disease.

Pray for others.

Be quick to forgive others of their wrongs and don't harbor unforgiveness in your heart.

Don't let the sun go down on your wrath (anger).

Build a stronghold of God's word in your heart and in your mind.

Guard your mouth and the words that come out of it.

Make sure the words you are speaking are full of life.

Keep the word of God before your eyes and in the midst of your heart always.

Make a point to laugh often.

Let go of stress in your life and replace it with peace.

Don't be anxious for nothing, but pray always.

Pray in your heavenly language for it knows what to pray.

Walk in and keep the commandment of love.

Love yourself and others.

Be quick to forgive, slow to speak, and quick to listen.

Confess your sins daily and ask for forgiveness.

Princess Bible Verse

Isaiah 53: 4-5

"Surely he has borne our griefs (sicknesses, weaknesses, and distresses) and carried our sorrows and pains [of punishment], yet we [ignorantly] considered him stricken, smitten, and afflicted by God [as if with leprosy]. But he was wounded for our transgressions, he was bruised for our guilt and iniquities; the chastisement [needful to obtain] peace and well-being for us was upon him, and with the stripes [that wounded] him we are healed and made whole."

👑 Princess Beauty Tips

A princess works hard at staying healthy both physically and spiritually, and she knows that reading the Bible will help keep both in shape. The word of God is referred to as medicine for the soul. When administered daily it can bring about healing and health to your bones. Take a dose of God's word every day.

👑 Princess Confessions

I have been redeemed from the curse of the law through the blood of Jesus. I am happy, healthy, and walking in healing.

👑 Princess Prayer

Lord, thank you for the benefits you have given to me and that you are the God who heals all my diseases and forgives all my iniquities. I pray that you will help me understand my God-given authority and the power I have over sickness and disease. Help me to walk in health and in healing, teach me how to take care of my body, and how to develop my faith. In Jesus' name, Amen.

👑 Princess Challenge

Read and study Deuteronomy 28 --the blessings and curses

👑 Princess Crown Thought

Dare to stay healthy and dare to believe God for your healing.

Princess Journaling Assignment

How much are you reading and studying the word of God? Do you really believe Jesus has paid the price for your sickness and disease, and His word has the ability to make you whole ? Write down the ways you can trust God for your healing.

Write Your Own Prayer:

Chapter 21

The Virtuous Woman

♛ Princess Bible Verse

Proverbs 31:30

"Charm and grace are deceptive, and beauty is vain [because it is not lasting], but a woman who reverently and worshipfully fears the Lord, she shall be praised!"

A virtuous woman does not waste her time, but she values every moment. She doesn't sit around on the couch reading romance novels or watching soap operas wishing and dreaming of a fairytale life. She creates a storybook of her own by the way she cares, tends, mends, loves, and nurtures her home, family, and husband. She works hard at everything she does and does it for the glory of her God. No task is too small or too large for her to handle. If she is cooking, cleaning, managing the finances, paying the bills, washing loads of laundry, or changing dirty diapers, she does it all with a smile.

A virtuous woman provides for her family and strives for excellence not only in the way she cares for herself, but also in the way she cares for her children, husband, family, friends, and the needy. It is not out of style or fashion for her to wear the apron and carry the load of being a mother or homemaker—a Domestic Engineer, as it has been labeled. A virtuous woman is more than a Domestic Engineer, she is a woman who loves her position no matter what the title—mother, wife, friend, lover, chef, comforter, cheerleader, chauffer, finance manager, home manger, interior decorator, seamstress, fitness buff, or laundry attendant. The virtuous woman is never lazy, always prepared and always strong in her spirit, body, and soul. She always has a kind word on her lips, a spring in her step, and a smile on her face. Does this woman ever have time to herself or ever feel tired? Yes, but she has learned to make time for herself and rest by creating balance in her lifestyle and responsibilities.

She knows who she is in her God and she knows her limitations. A virtuous woman is a woman of victory, and in her victorious state, she keeps a guard on the gates of weariness. She knows when she needs to rest, and she knows when to say no.

This woman of excellence knows the importance of drawing from her God. She visits with him on a regular basis and keeps him in the midst of her heart and mind. When she needs energy, she draws from him. When she needs wisdom, she relies on him. When she needs encouragement, she is confident he will supply. A virtuous woman is a visionary, a missionary in her own field, an optimistic and cheerful thinker, a giver, caregiver, and a generous woman at heart. She is a woman of influence, a woman of great courage and strength. Excellence, honor, and integrity make her shine in a world of darkness, sin, and unrighteousness.

She sets the atmosphere of her home and character by the colors she chooses to express. The wallpaper of her heart and home are textured, colored, and pasted on with love. A virtuous woman only speaks words of peace, joy, victory, love, health, and life unto herself, to her family, and to others around her. Love is the source of her strength which keeps her moving, caring, acting, and living. The reverential fear of her God, the love he sheds abroad in her heart, and the tender way he calls her his own, keeps, protects, and preserves her in becoming all she has been purposed to be in the heart of God.

God loves the virtuous woman, and desires her to come to the place he has created for her to live. God will always love her unconditionally, just as he would any of his children. A virtuous woman's beauty never fades, and she always eats from the good of the land. Her husband loves, adores, protects, and praises her. Her children rise up and call her blessed. She causes no one evil, never gossips, backbites, shows jealousy, envy, or anger. She never holds unforgiveness in her heart toward anyone but instead prays for them. She is quick to repent of her sin and makes prayer a part of her daily life.

The virtuous woman is a special daughter of God because she chooses to live her life for the God she loves and for the family he so dearly blessed her with.

Every woman has the opportunity to become the virtuous woman mentioned in Proverbs 10:31. It is a choice. John 3:16 in the Amplified Bible says, God greatly loves and dearly prizes us. God prizes all his children. However, there is something special about a virtuous woman that makes her stand out in the sight of God.

Princess Beauty Tips

A gold medal is an award of excellence. A princess always wears a gold medal of excellence draped around her neck as a reminder of her excellent spirit. God rewards those who diligently seek him. God will reward you for having a spirit of excellence and a reverential fear for him.

Princess Confessions

I choose to be a woman of excellence and will reflect the beauty of my Father who lives in me. I will fear the Lord and walk in his ways.

Princess Prayer

Father, what a blessing it is to be a woman and what a greater blessing it is to be called your daughter. Help me to become like the virtuous woman and become a woman of excellence, beauty, and strength. In Jesus' name, Amen.

Princess Challenge

Become a woman of true beauty and excellent by the ways you choose to live your life every day.

Princess Crown Thought

A virtuous woman is far more precious than jewels, and her value is far above rubies or pearls.

Princess Journaling Assignment

Can you compare yourself to the virtuous woman? How can you become more like her? Make a list of the things you can improve in your life to become more like her.

_____
_____
_____
_____
_____
_____
_____
_____

Write Your Own Prayer:

_____
_____
_____
_____
_____
_____
_____
_____

Chapter 22

God and Queen Esther

👑 Princess Bible Verse

Esther 4:14

"For if you keep silent at this time, relief and deliverance shall arise for the Jews from elsewhere, but you and your father's house will perish. And who knows but that you have come to the kingdom for such a time as this and for this very occasion?"

The book of Esther is found in the Old Testament. It is a book that tells of a wonderful woman of God who is beautiful, smart, and courageous. Esther is a wonderful book that teaches us the importance of staying true to God and being obedient to his commands. It shows us that a willing vessel can do mighty works for God. Esther was an ordinary woman and God took her and used her in a way that history will not let us forget. God is no respecter of person, and what he did through Esther he can also do through you, if you are willing.

Esther was a young child when she lost her parents and almost everyone in her family. They were Jews, and in those days, it was not fashionable to be a Jew. Therefore, the wicked in the providences sought to kill all the Jews they could find. Esther's life could have been over, but God rescued her through the love of a relative. Mordecai, her cousin, saved Esther from her devastation, took her into his home, and raised her as his own daughter. Mordecai was also a Jew and saved by God to help complete the calling on Esther's life.

As you read the book of Esther and listen closely, you will find Jesus in the middle of the story. Mordecai took and loved, raised, taught, encouraged, comforted, and gave Esther a chance at life. That is what Jesus did for you. You were not a member of his family, but he grafted you in by dying on the cross for your sins. He did not have to die for you, but he loved you so much he gave up his life. By his blood, he has given you a hope. By his spirit, he has given you the opportunity to be taught by the best, encouraged, strengthened, and comforted.

You may feel as if you have lost everything in your life, your family, your will to go on, your self-worth, and your place in this world. But God has given everything you have lost, back to you in one gift, his son Jesus. Jesus is the only way to life, health, and restoration. Run to him, hug him, and let him take you in as his own.

Esther grew up in a Jewish home and was taught all the Jewish traditions and beliefs. Mordecai made sure she knew how important it was to serve God and to stay true to him. Esther did not know at the time how valuable all her life lessons would be. Esther was a beautiful woman not only on the outside, but also on the inside. She knew who she was and she knew her God. She loved God with all her heart and wanted to obey him.

Beauty is not the only thing in life that will get you places. But what is on the inside of that beauty will take you places you will never go on your natural beauty. The beauty of the spirit will take you on the time of your life. Esther's beauty on the inside made her into a woman of good character. You can be beautiful on the outside but ugly on the inside; Esther knew good character would give her favor beyond her natural ability. She was known in her community as being a woman beautiful, kind, and faithful to God and her family.

The story goes on to tell us that King Xerxes ordered his officers in all the provinces of his kingdom to gather all beautiful young woman and bring them to his palace. The officers followed the king's orders and brought all the beautiful woman to him. Now, Esther was among those beautiful women taken to the palace. There is no record of her fighting the officers. She went willingly. Sometimes you can fight the perfect will of God by fighting your way through life. You want to do it your way and not God's way, so you fight. When you see your life not going anywhere, stop and ask yourself, am I fighting against God's plan? When you stop fighting against God, hold his hand and stop pushing it away, he will lead you places you could have never gotten to on your own. It is not worth fighting against God to have your own way.

God's way is so much better for your life. He already knows the roads you need to go down to reach your destination. Let go of your selfish ambitions and let God take you to those ambitions you never knew existed. God can only use a willing vessel. He will never go against your will.

When Esther arrived at the king's palace, she immediately found favor in the sight of all. That divine favor granted her the best room in the palace, special treatment, the choice (best) maidservants, and insight to the king's likes and dislikes. Favor will take you when nothing else will. True favor comes from God. He is the author of favor. When you start serving God, favor will follow you everywhere you go.

It is also interesting to see that she had the very best in the palace. Favor produces the best. God always knows the best for your life and for your well-being. Esther had the best. She was loved and accepted, especially by those in authority. When you have God on the inside, he will produce the favor on the outside. When you carry the beauty of Christ, he covers you as a shield with his divine, outstanding favor.

After all the woman were gathered and brought to the palace, they were assigned twelve months of beauty preparations before they could ever see the king. Each woman had to undergo treatments,: six months with oil of myrrh, six months with perfumes, and preparations for beautifying women. They had to be prepared properly before they could continue with the selection process. King Xerxes wanted a queen who was prepared.

In life, you have grown accustomed to fast, easy, and instant results. But instant results are not always how things come to pass. Sometimes we have to learn the virtue of patience. Patience is a part of being successful. If you rush into something without first preparing for it, you may be setting yourself up for failure. Wisdom is the key and time has its perfect work. God takes you through seasons in your life. He has you in school for a season, or he may have you work a certain job for a season. Whatever the case or the place, there is a plan underlying the season. Everything you do in life prepares you for the next step and the next step. Never question why you may be doing something, instead pray for peace in the situation until God brings you through.

Esther was patient and God brought her through. She showed herself faithful and took heed to the instructions given. You may not want to take heed (obey, listen, do) to the instructions God has given you through his word or through another person. But to stay on course, you must always be willing to listen, do, and obey instructions.

Esther again found favor, but this time it was in the eyes of the king. Esther had the option to take anything with her when she was permitted to see the king—gold and silver jewelry, fine linens, shoes, etc. However, she chose to take with her what she already had—her beauty, charm, poise, and grace. The king was captivated. Esther had all the confidence she needed to see the king. She didn't need any earthly treasure to make her beauty shine, because the most important treasure was hidden inside her heart—the divine beauty of God.

When it is time for you to step out and to step forth into your destiny, don't take anything with you but your faith. Your God is the only precious jewel you will ever need to get someone's attention. Captivate your audience with the presence of God in your life.

Esther found grace and favor with the king. The first time he laid eyes on her, he knew something was different. Not only did her natural beauty glow in the lights of the palace room, but so did her confidence. The king fell in love with her, made Esther queen, and placed a royal crown on her head. Esther was truly blessed by the king with good and perfect gifts.

God loves you and knew you from the beginning of time. The moment he set his eyes and thoughts on you, he loved you. You have favor and grace in God's eyes. You are beautiful to him all the time. Even when you mess up and get out of relationship with him, he still loves you. God longs for a personal relationship with you. Jesus has crowned you with his beauty and with his love. You are royalty through Christ Jesus. You are a princess in the sight of God. The King of Kings, Jesus Christ, is your heavenly Father. Just as Esther was crowned as princess of the kingdom, so have you been crowned a princess in the kingdom of God.

Esther had wonderful gifts given to her. She did not ask for them, they were granted to her according to the king's pleasure. God has granted you gifts—you were not crowned without them. He has given you his Son, Jesus, as a gift of eternal life. He didn't have to let his son die for your sins, but he did it out of love. Jesus lives today because he loves you. He has given you the most precious gift anyone could have ever given, his life—so you could have life.

God has also given you gifts and talents, prosperity, healing, the Holy Spirit, and spiritual gifts. When the King gives out gifts, he only gives out the best. You are gifted for the kingdom of God. Don't use your talents and gifting to gain position and acceptance in this world. Instead, use them for God's glory and you will be exalted in due time.

Esther was blessed by the king with good and perfect gifts and so are you blessed with the same. For God's gifts and his call are irrevocable. [He never withdraws them when once they are given, and he does not change his mind about those to who he gives his grace or to whom he sends his call], (Romans 11:29). You are a gift of God to this earth for such a time as this.

Esther went on to save a nation of Jews from being destroyed. She saved a people that were dear to God's heart. God knew exactly what he was doing, he had a plan in place, and Esther happened to be part of the plan. God has a plan for your life. He is no respecter of person, what he has done for others he will do for you. Just as Esther saved her people, so are you destined to save a lost and dying world to Christ Jesus, your people, God's people. His kingdom will one day rule and reign on this earth.

Don't you want to live in the king's palace? Although King Xerxes had no prior knowledge of Esther, he knew she was destined for greatness. One night with the king set her up to fulfill the calling God placed on her life. She was made a part of the Kingdom for a reason, as you have been set on this earth and into Gods' Kingdom, for such a time as this.

The Character of Esther

Beautiful, lovely, kind, respectful, gentle, obedient, quick to obey and to heed instruction, bold, courageous, victorious, loved, cherished, self-confident, established, rooted and grounded, blessed beyond measure, a daughter of God, highly favored, and destined for greatness

♛ Princess Beauty Tips

A princess wears her crown with dignity and honor and understands the authority that has been given with it. The crown is worn on the head as a symbol of authority and power. Wear the crown of authority God has given you and walk in the benefits of your position.

♛ Princess Confessions

I am a member of the royal family of Christ Jesus; I have been made a princess and crowned with beauty and splendor. I have been born for such a time as this.

♛ Princess Prayer

Thank you, Father, for crowning me with your beauty and splendor and calling me your own. I am so thankful you have brought me to yourself and called me by my name. Your word says you have my picture on the palm of your hand. Thank you for giving me life through your son, Jesus, and allowing me to become a bearer of light for him. I pray you will help me keep my foot on the path of righteousness so that I can be as Queen Esther, highly favored, blessed beyond measure, and beautiful inside and out. In Jesus' name, Amen.

♛ Princess Challenge

I challenge you to recognize the importance of being a woman and determine in your heart to be all the woman God has created you to be. You have been born for such a time as this, and you are destined to accomplish great things for the Lord and his Kingdom.

♛ Princess Crown Thought

Don't waste time being something you are not. Instead, take hold of the things of God and run with them. He needs you!

Princess Journaling Assignment

Why do you think God has called you for such a time as this? Do you think you are capable of doing the things Esther did to save her people? What are you doing to help spread the kingdom of Christ on earth? Do you believe you are destined for greatness? Why or why not?

_____

_____

_____

_____

_____

_____

_____

_____

_____

_____

_____

_____

_____

_____

_____

_____

_____

Write Your Own Prayer:

Princess Beauty Treatments

Deep Hair Conditioner

1 avocado, peeled and mashed

Light coconut milk

*Mash ingredients together to form the texture of shampoo, apply to the hair, and leave on for up to twenty minutes. This is a messy recipe, cover clothes with a towel or apply while sitting in a warm bath.

Hair Mask

1 cup purified water

1 banana

1 tbs plain yogurt

1 tbs honey

1 cup cantaloupe

1 tbs condensed milk

1 tsp wheat germ oil

*Mix ingredients in a blender and apply to dry hair. Start at the roots and leave on for up to forty-five minutes, rinse, and shampoo.

Body-Boosting Hair Treatment

4 tbs lemon juice

1 med. avocado

1 tbs blackstrap molasses

*Mix all ingredients until smooth and apply to dry hair. Leave on for up to twenty minutes, rinse, and shampoo.

Paraffin Hand Treatment

1 lb. paraffin wax

Glass bowl

*Chop up paraffin and microwave to melt, stir, and let set until warm. Smear wax over hands, and let dry about ten minutes. Cover your hands with latex gloves and top with oven mitts. Peel the wax off once it has dried to hands and replace back into a container to be reused.

Oatmeal Hand Treatment

2 cups of powdered oatmeal

4 tbs honey

4 tbs water

*Mix together and apply to top of hands. Let mixture dry and rinse. Apply lotion to secure the moisture. If mixture is too thick, add water to thin.

Face Moisture Mask

1 avocado

1 cup olive oil

*Peel, pit, and smash avocado. Mix with olive oil until smooth. Apply and rinse after thirty to forty minutes. Good for dry to normal skin.

Face Scrub #1

1 cup finely chopped almonds

1 cup honey

2 to 3 drops of lemon juice

*Mix ingredients to make a paste. Rub gently to exfoliate the skin. Leave mixture on for about five to ten minutes. Rinse and rub gently, especially the area around your nose, between your brows, and on your chin. This mixture is great for unclogging pores, removing, and preventing blackheads.

Face Scrub #2

1 cup of white or brown sugar

Water

*Mix ingredients together to form a paste. Rub mixture gently onto skin in circular motions. Avoid the eye area. Rinse well and place remaining sugar mixture in an air-tight container.

Oatmeal and Egg Mask

1 cup powdered oatmeal

1 to 2 egg whites at room temperature

1 cup of water

*Mix ingredients until blended. If mixture is to thin, add more oatmeal. If mixture is too thick, add more water. Leave mixture on face for up to twenty minutes, or until it is good and dry. This mask is good for normal to oily skin. Use before bedtime once a week.

Body Scrub #1

2 to 3 fresh peaches at room temperature

1 cup brown sugar

2 cups of almond oil or baby oil

*Blend peaches, brown sugar and oil until peaches are well blended. While in the shower without the water on, apply scrub to all of body. Do not apply to face if you have oily skin. Leave on for as long as you desire.

Body Scrub #2

granulated sea salt

almond oil

Mix equal amounts together to form a scrub. Apply the mixture to a wet washrag and rub entire body gently. Store remaining scrub in an air-tight container next to the shower or tub. This can be used as often as you wish.

Face Mask for Oily Skin

1 tsp lemon juice

Note: If you have a real lemon, squeeze the juice along with some pulp into your recipe.

2 egg whites

2 tsp honey

1 cup of strawberries

*If you are making this recipe for only one person, cut recipe in half. Blend ingredients, apply to face and neck, leave on for ten minutes, then rinse. The juices from lemons and strawberries are natural astringents.

Face Mask for Normal Skin

Clay from a health food store

Note: clay from the Dead Sea works the best

1 tsp honey

Water (for a richer mask, use whole milk)

*Mix two parts water to one part clay, mixing in honey, add more water if clay is too dry. Apply to the face and neck area, and leave on for fifteen minutes. Rinse off with a warm washcloth or simply get into the shower. Clay is a great skin hydrator and toner. You can find clay at a health food store. Clay has been dated back to the days of Cleopatra.

Face Mask for Dry Skin

1 avocado

1 cup honey

Peel avocado, remove seed, mash, and add honey. Apply to face and neck and leave on for five to ten minutes. Rinse. Avocados and honey are natural moisturizers.

Face Mask for Combination Skin

6 rose petals

2 tbsp rosewater

1 tbsp plain yogurt

1 tbsp runny honey

Note: warm honey to make runny, make sure you don't get it scolding hot and burn it

*Tear rose petals into tiny pieces and soak in water until petals become good and soggy, add yogurt, and honey. Mix well and apply to face and neck. Leave on for about ten minutes, then rinse. The oil in rose petals is a natural skin balancer.

Face Mask for Sensitive Skin

1 cup plain yogurt (good and cold)

1 cup powdered oatmeal

*Mix ingredients together to form a paste, apply to the skin, and leave on for about fifteen minutes. This is a great mask for chapped, sunburned, or irritated skin. You can also use this recipe for other skin types. For oily skin, add drops of lime or lemon juice. For dry to normal skin, add in a tablespoon of honey.

Five Minute Foot Care

Mix one-third cup of uncooked instant oatmeal and 1/2 cup of your favorite body cream. Rub into heels, soles, and toes, then rinse off. Next, layer on a light coat of olive or almond oil, and slip your feet into a favorite pair of cotton socks. Put your feet up and relax a few minutes while the oils and lotions do their work. Remove your socks and feel the softness right away, or sleep in them and discover the softness when you awake.

I personally love using homemade recipes. I never spend a lot of money on expensive skincare products. If any of the above recipes feel uncomfortable on the skin, wash them off quickly. Test each ingredient in the recipe on the inside of your wrist for signs of irritation. Beauty recipe books were very common in early history. The books were passed down from generation to generation, just like a precious heirloom. Not only did the books contain beauty recipes, but they also included home remedies for sickness and other ailments.

Keeping your body healthy and looking beautiful from crown to toe, use these three ingredients:

1. Commitment
2. Consistency
3. Careful Attention

Prayer for Salvation

Father in heaven, I come to you in the name of Jesus. I am asking you to save me by forgiving me of my sins. I confess that Jesus is Lord and believe that he died and rose again. I ask you to live in my heart and be the Lord of my life. Thank you for saving me. In Jesus' name, Amen. *CONFESS*--I am saved and the redeemed of God! Scripture reference: John 1:12; 3:16, II Corinthians 5:17, Romans 10:9-10, and Ephesians 2:8-9.

Prayer for Assignment

Father, I thank you that (I) have been given a gift and assignment from heaven. I pray that the unique abilities that you have placed in (me) will make room for (me) and bring (me) before the great leaders of our day. I pray that (I) will walk in accuracy and obedience to your complete and perfect will. I know that when you saved (me), you also called (me) with a holy and distinct calling. Help (me) to faithfully develop (my) talents and tools in such a way that you may be glorified in the entire world. In the name of Jesus. Amen.

Scripture Reference: Proverbs 18:16, Isaiah 1:19, and II Timothy 1:9

Prayer for Protection

Father, I thank you that (I) have a refuge and a fortress of protection in you. No evil shall come upon (me), neither will any sickness, diseases, or tragedy come near to (my) dwelling. Thank you for commissioning your angels to guard, protect, and defend (me) from all harm. I pray that no weapon that is designed against (me) will succeed, and every tongue that would rise up against (me) be silenced in the name of Jesus Christ. Scripture Reference: Psalm 91:1, 10-11, Isaiah 54:17, and Hebrews 1:13-14

Prayer for Boldness

Father, I thank you for giving me the spirit of boldness as I walk with you. I pray that the power of the Holy Spirit will rise up within me to be the witness for Christ that you want me to be. I pray that I will never be ashamed of the Gospel, but I will realize that it's the power of God to save and deliver hurting people. Thank you, Father that I do not operate with fear or apprehension, but I am bold as a lion, possessing strength, confidence, and a steadfast mind. In Jesus' name. Amen

Scripture Reference: Acts 1:8, Romans 1:16, II Timothy 1:7, and Proverbs 28:1

Prayer for Wisdom

Father, thank you for giving me the spirit of wisdom and revelation. My head is covered with the helmet of salvation, and I have the mind of Christ. I pray that I will make intelligent, informed, and spirit-inspired decisions today. I pray to enjoy supernatural discernment and make clever evaluations of every situation I encounter. In Jesus' name, I pray, Amen.

Scripture Reference: Ephesians 1:17, 6:17, and I Corinthians 2:16

Prayer for Favor

Father, I thank you that I am blessed of God, and surrounded with his shield of favor. I pray that throughout the day people will want to bless, assist, and encourage me. I believe that I will enjoy unusual cooperation and overwhelming goodwill in all my activities. As I walk in your favor with you, I thank you for complimenting me with favor and promotion from people. In Jesus' name, Amen.

Scripture Reference: Psalm 91:1, 10-11, Isaiah 54:17, and Hebrews 1:13-14

Prayer for Strength

Father, I thank you for giving me a spirit of might and extraordinary strength to resist temptation and to stand strong against the schemes of the devil. I pray that I will stand today, fully clothed in the armor of God, and successfully stop and extinguish every dart fired by my enemy. I thank you for I have focused my eyes on Jesus, and I am looking to his word. I thank you that I am strong, your word lives and endures in me and I have overcome and completely conquered the wicked one. In Jesus' name, Amen.

Scripture Reference: Ephesians 3:16, 6:11; I John 2:14)

Prayer for Freedom from Bondage to Food

Father, I come to you in the name of Jesus Christ. I know that Jesus paid the sacrifice so we might be free. This freedom allows me to be free from obesity and unhealthy eating habits. I know you have given me one body in this lifetime to take care of and value with respect. Lord, I am asking you to guide and direct me when it comes to staying healthy and in shape. I confess that I will make an effort to stay physically fit and healthy. I pray that you will reveal to me the areas of my eating habits that need to be changed. I want to complete the call you have placed on my life and I know I must stay healthy in order to complete it. I ask for your help to resist the temptation to overeat and become lazy. In Jesus' name, Amen.

Write Your Own Prayer:

_____

_____

_____

_____

_____

_____

_____

_____

_____

_____

Beauty and the Bible

Beautiful

Gen. 29:17; Deut. 21:11; I Sam. 16:12, 25:3; 2 Sam. 11:2; Est. 2:7; Ps. 48:2; Eccl. 3:11; Song. 5:4, 7:1; Is. 4:2, 52:1, 52:7, 64:11; Jer. 13:20, 48:17; Eze. 65:12, 23:42; Mat. 23:27; Acts 3:2, 3:10; Rom. 10:15

Beauty

Ex. 28:2, 28:40; 2 Sam.1:19, 17:25; 1 Chr. 16:29, 2 Chr. 3:6, 20:21; Est. 1:11; Job 40:10; Ps. 27:4, 29:2, 39:11, 45:11, 49:17, 50:2, 90:17, 96:6, 96:9; Prov. 6:25, 20:29, 31:30; Is. 3:24, 13:19, 28:1, 28:4, 16:14; Eze. 16:15, 16:25, 27:3, 27:4, 27:11, 28:7, 28:12, 28:17, 31:8, 32:19; Hos. 14:6; Zec. 9:17, 11:7, 11:10

Beautiful Women of the Bible

Sarah, Genesis 12

Rebekah, Genesis 24

Rachel, Genesis 29

Daughters of Job, Job 42

Abigail, I Samuel 25

Bath-Sheba, II Samuel 11

Tamar, II Samuel 13

Abishag, I Kings 1

Vashti, Esther 1

Esther, the book of Esther

The Ten Commandments

Exodus Chapter 20

1. You shall have no other Gods before me.
2. You shall not make yourself a carved image.
3. You shall not bear false witness.
4. You shall not kill.
5. You shall not steal.
6. Honor your mother and your father.
7. Keep the Sabbath day holy.
8. You shall not covet.
9. You shall not commit adultery.
10. You shall not take the name of the Lord your God in vain.

The Fruit of the Spirit

"But the fruit of the [Holy] Spirit [the work which his presence within accomplishes] is love, joy (gladness), peace, patience (an even temper, forbearance), kindness, goodness (benevolence), faithfulness, gentleness (meekness, humility), self-control (self-restraint, continence). Against such things there is no law [that can bring a charge]."

Galatians 5:22-23

When you accept Jesus into your heart and make him Lord over your life, you are not only forgiven of your sins, but you are also made new with his character traits. Your old sinful nature has been washed away and has been replaced with a new nature, the nature of God. The fruit of the spirit are characteristics of God's nature. God wants you to act like him so you can be witnesses to others. As you grow and mature into an adult believer, your soul should also be prospering. You can tell if your soul is prospering by the fruit it is producing. Let the presence of God's character take over your life.

Fruit of the Spirit

Love	Joy	Peace
Patience	Kindness	Goodness
Faithfulness	Gentleness	Self-control

Princess Charm School: A Godly Approach to Beauty, Poise, and Righteousness

Princess Review

Choose from the following words to complete each question.
heart, fearfully and wonderfully, self-confidence, royal, mirror, unconditionally, Queen Esther, false, seated, natural and spiritual, false, delight, acknowledge, armor, false, true,

Man looks at the outward appearance but God cares about the appearance of your _____.

Psalm 139:14 says, I am _____ and _____ made!

God-confidence will enhance your _____.

You are a member of the _____ family.

God's word is like a _____ reflecting the light of Jesus into your life.

God loves me _____.

_____ was a beautiful woman that God used to save a nation of people.

You have been _____ in heavenly places with Christ Jesus.

What are the two types of correct posture?

1. In the _____
2. In the _____

Princess Review |253

Give two examples of how you can mind your manners.

1. _____

2. _____

A princess should take a bath once a week.   True or False.

Define true beauty.

_____

_____

_____ yourself in the Lord and he will give you the desires and secret petitions of your heart. Psalm 37:4

_____ the Lord in all your ways and he will lead, guide, and direct your paths. Proverbs 3:6

Put on the full _____ of God.

Wearing clothes that reveal a lot of skin is pleasing in the sight of God. True or False

You have been created in the image of God. You are a one-of-a-kind divine design.   True or False.

Name the ten commandments.

1. _____
2. _____
3. _____
4. _____
5. _____
6. _____
7. _____
8. _____
9. _____
10. _____

Define the fruits of the spirit.

Love _____

Joy _____

Peace _____

Goodness _____

Kindness _____

Patience _____

Faithfullness _____

Gentleness _____

Self-control _____

Declaration of Acceptance

I _____
have successfully read Princess Charm School in its entirety. I understand that I am a special and unique creation of God, created for his pleasure and goodness. I understand that I am a member of the royal family of Jesus Christ and as His daughter; I am a royal princess. I declare to live my life in a way that is pleasing and acceptable before the Father's eyes. I will walk, talk, dress, and behave accordingly. I also understand that God loves me unconditionally and it is by His divine love that I am divinely beautiful.

Declared this _____ day of _____, _____.

Signed:
Princess _____

Endnotes

Chapter 1--...and God Created Woman--1. Excerpts taken from the Holy Bible, Woman Thou Art Loose Edition, Copyright@ 1998 by Thomas Nelson, Inc. Used by permission.

Chapter 3--True Beauty-- 1. The American Heritage High School Dictionary. --4th ed. Copyright @ 2002 Houghton Mifflin C company. All rights reserved.; 2. Genesis 1:26; 3. I Corinthians 6:19; 4. Matthew 22:14

Chapter 4--God and Your Body, Soul, and Spirit--1. Huston, Susan. Runway to Beauty Handbook; 2. Psalm 139:14

Chapter 5--God and Exercise
1. U.S. Dept of Agriculture and the U.S. Dept of Health and Human Services. Copyright 1998 National Cattlemen's Beef Association

Chapter 8--God and Your Hair--1. Matthew 10:30; 2. I Corinthians 11:15; 3. Huston, Susan. Runway to Beauty Handbook

Chapter 9--God and Your Hands and Feet--1. Mark 16:18; 2. Matthew 7:8

Chapter 10--God and Your Smile--1. James 1:17; 2. Proverbs 4:23

Chapter 11--God in Your Closet--1. Genesis 1:27; 2. Proverbs 3:5-6

Chapter 12--All About Me--1. I John 4:19

Chapter 13--God and Your Posture--1. Philippians 3:14; 2. II Peter 1:3; 3. Luke 10:19; 4. Genesis 1:28; 5. Ephesians 1:20

Chapter 14--God and Your Confidence--1. Proverbs 13:12; 2. Nehemiah 8:10; 3. Philippians 4:13

Chapter 16--God and the Fashion Industry--1. Genesis 3:21; 2. Isaiah 14

Chapter 18--God and Righteousness--1. The American Heritage High School Dictionary. --4th ed. Copyright @ 2002 Houghton Mifflin Company; 2. Romans 6:23; 3. II Corinthians 5:21; 4. Hebrews 5:13; 5. Romans 10:17; 6. Hebrews 5:13-14; 7. Psalm 119:11; 8. Galatians 5:16; 9. Philippians 4:8

Chapter 19--God and Your Relationships--1. Proverbs 18:24; 2. John 20:29; 3. Exodus 20:5; 4. Mark 7:13; 5. James 4:2

Chapter 20--God and Your Future--1. III John 2; 2. Philippians 4:13;

Chapter 21--God and Your Healing--1. Romans 10:17; 2. III John 2

Lisa Delmedico Harris is an author and speaker whose passion is to teach and encourage women of all ages to be the best they can be. For more information about Lisa's books or speaking ministry, to learn more about Princess Charm School, its outreaches, curriculum, products and services, to sign up for mailings, or to share how God has used this book in your life, please contact Lisa or visit her website.

Contact Author

Lisa Delmedico Harris

7511 E 243 Str. So.

Porum, Oklahoma 74455

Email: lisa@princesscharmschool.com

Or Visit: www.princesscharmschool.com

BOOKS BY LISA:

To learn more about books and other resources, visit:
https://www.princesscharmschool.com/shop

Join the Academy and continue your Princess Charm School journey. Joining, grants you access to an exclusive social, etiquette and life skills academy designed to equip you with tools to help you
Sparkle in all areas of your life.

To learn more about this exclusive academy, visit,
https://www.princesscharmschool.com/academy-princess-charm-school

Lisa Delmedico Harris

Manners Never Go Out Of Style

Thank you for reading Princess Charm School: A Godly Approach to Beauty, Poise, and Righteousness

Made in United States
Orlando, FL
17 February 2024